9: Nuclear Politics: America, France, and Britain

THE WASHINGTON PAPERS
Volume I

9: Nuclear Politics: America, France, and Britain

Wynfred Joshua
and
Walter F. Hahn

THE CENTER FOR STRATEGIC AND INTERNATIONAL STUDIES
Georgetown University, Washington, D.C.

SAGE PUBLICATIONS
Beverly Hills / London

For information address:

SAGE PUBLICATIONS, INC.
275 South Beverly Drive
Beverly Hills, California 90212

SAGE PUBLICATIONS LTD
St George's House / 44 Hatton Garden
London EC1N 8ER

International Standard Book Number 0-8039-0282-4

Library of Congress Catalog Card No. 73-83411

FIRST PRINTING

*When citing a Washington Paper, please use the proper form. Remember to cite
the series title and include the paper number. One of the two following formats
can be adapted (depending on the style manual used):*

(1) HASSNER, P. (1973) "Europe in the Age of Negotiation." The Washington
Papers, I, 8. Beverly Hills and London: Sage Pubns.

OR

(2) Hassner, Pierre. 1973. *Europe in the Age of Negotiation.* The Washington
Papers, vol. 1, no. 8. Beverly Hills and London: Sage Publications.

CONTENTS

The Nuclear Aspect of Anglo-French Relations

For more than 20 years, the strength undergirding the Atlantic alliance has been American nuclear supremacy and the conviction in Western Europe that the U.S. strategic arsenal would, when necessary, be invoked in the defense of the North Atlantic alliance. A chain of developments, highlighted by the advent of nuclear parity between the United States and the Soviet Union, has cast doubt on the validity of what has been popularly characterized as the "American guarantee." The doubts have been exacerbated by a number of trends and events in the past decade, particularly the growing introversion of American politics in the wake of frustration in Vietnam, the audible pressures in the United States for stinting the American military presence in Europe, and such superpower accommodations as in SALT I. These European doubts are, to be sure, of long standing. America's allies in Europe have always harbored the fear that one day the United States might turn its back upon Europe. Shortly after World War II, Britain and France perceived the need for insurance against precisely this contingency. The decisions by both countries to create nuclear forces of their own were animated strongly by this perception.

AUTHORS' NOTE: *The authors gratefully acknowledge the encouragement of Richard B. Foster, Director of the Strategic Studies Center, Stanford Research Institute, in writing this study. They take pleasure in thanking Albert Ferri, Jr. for his support in preparing the section on*

The nuclear credentials of Great Britain and France—no matter how modest these may be by superpower standards—are by now clearly established. In the light of strategic nuclear parity at the superpower level, of perceived trends in the United States, and of rapid shifts in the international environment more generally, there has been renewed speculation about the possible emergence of a Western European nuclear deterrent based upon Anglo-French nuclear cooperation.

It is the purpose of this study to examine the possibility of such cooperation and to weigh the implications for the Western alliance and particularly for the policies of the United States.

American political and legal barriers to nuclear sharing. The authors also extend their appreciation to the Center for Strategic and International Studies, Georgetown University, for including this work in its new Washington Papers series. This study is based on independent research and was originally undertaken as one of a series of projects supported by the External Research Program of the U.S. Department of State. The authors are solely responsible for the analyses and conclusions, which do not represent the official views of the U.S. government or the Department of State; nor do they reflect the views of the Stanford Research Institute or the Center for Strategic and International Studies.

French and British Strategic Predilections

A comparison of the mainstreams of French and British strategic thinking reveals marked similarities as well as differences. Both France and Great Britain have been steadfast in stressing the need for maintaining national nuclear forces. But the British rationale, unlike that of the French, generally has not assigned to British forces a role that is basically independent of the strategic forces of the United States. Thus, unlike the French, the British have coordinated the targeting of their nuclear forces with the strike plans of NATO.

Both the French and the British concepts of nuclear strategy were shaped in the early postwar years by strategic thinkers who emphasized the utility of early strategic retaliation against the enemy's urban centers. But the French, unlike the British, have gradually modified this old doctrine in favor of a more varied and sophisticated strategy.

French and British Perceptions of the Military Threat

Both France and Britain tend to emphasize the political dimensions of the overall threat to Western Europe. Until the mid-1960s when the American government sought to justify a strategy for NATO that stressed a conventional defense, the threat of a deliberate and massive sweep of Warsaw Pact forces across Western Europe had been kept in the forefront of NATO planning. The French and British, however, had long before largely discounted this extreme contingency, partly because of their own estimates of Soviet intentions, and partly because of their concepts of nuclear deterrence. French and British strategic planners assigned greater probability and priority to the dangers of (1) Soviet exploitation of military power for political coercion, and (2) a conflict escalating from a crisis.

The fears in Paris and London of Soviet political coercion accord with an overall conception, in both capitals, in which stability is equated with military balance on the continent and, conversely, imbalance is seen as the agent of destabilizing actions. French and British leaders have voiced the fear that the Soviet Union, if it were to achieve clear-cut military superiority in Europe, would harness this superiority to a campaign of subtle political pressures and intimidation aimed at establishing hegemony over Western Europe. In essence, this is the specter of "Finlandization" that has gained more general currency in Europe in recent years. The fear of neutralization of Western Europe under the shadow of Soviet military superiority goes far to explain the skepticism in Paris and London about mutual balanced force reductions (MBFR) and the insistence in both countries that American troops in Europe be maintained at their present levels.

French and British preoccupation with the political dimensions of the military threat, however, does not exclude the notion that the threat to Western Europe may, under certain circumstances, assume direct military dimensions. The direct military threat is seen in both countries largely as the concomitant of crisis and its possible escalation. This contingency was underscored by the Soviet intervention in Czechoslovakia in 1968. The developments in Czechoslovakia seemed to give more urgency to the likelihood that a crisis internal to the Warsaw Pact could spill over into a greater European conflagration.

In Paris particularly, the events of August 1968 and their aftermath evoked some unusual reactions. Thus, although the French maintained their official aloofness from Nato, the allied commanders in Europe found their French military counterparts markedly more cooperative, if "unofficially" so, after those events (Kohl, 1971: 263). Simultaneously, French strategists seemed to pay more attention to the possibilities of conflict on the Central Front and to reject the so-called all-azimuths threat.[1] Moreover, it was in late 1968 that apprehensions began to be voiced in Paris over the possibility of U.S. troop withdrawals from Europe. These apprehensions contrasted starkly with the earlier Gaullist theme that forecast the inevitability of American reductions.[2]

The British, for their part, stepped up conspicuously their support to NATO after the Czech crisis.[3] The steadily improving Soviet capability in Europe fueled fears in London of drastic shifts in the regional balance of power—witness the somber statements by the then British Defense Minister, Denis Healey (1969), about NATO being outnumbered on the Central Front by more than two to one in infantry and nearly three to one in armor. The fears of the Labour government were partly reflected in British support for the creation of the NATO Eurogroup as an institutional means of fashioning a security consensus among the European members of the alliance.

French and British apprehensions of unpremeditated conflict extend beyond the Central region. The growing Soviet naval intrusion into the Mediterranean has been viewed with some anxiety in Paris and London, not only as a threat to the residual interests of the two countries in the Mediterranean and Middle Eastern affairs, but also as the possible harbinger of conflict triggered by U.S.-Soviet confrontation. French concerns have been mirrored in France's increased participation in NATO air surveillance and naval maneuvers in the Mediterranean (Kohl, 1971: 263). British trepidations can be detected in the decision of the Conservative government to override that of its predecessor and retain a small British naval and air presence in the Indian Ocean.

There are other, less publicized dimensions in the threat perceptions of France and Great Britain. Thus the danger of internal subversion apparently continues to occupy some attention in London and Paris. Particularly the French are concerned that in the event of conflict a sabotage campaign might be directed by French Communists and other subversive elements against France's nuclear establishment.[4]

There is another item that must be included in any discussion of the "threats" as seen from Paris and London, and this concerns the role and power of West Germany. To be sure, some 27 years of postwar reconciliation have dampened French and British fears of a renaissance of German militarism. Certainly, a "German military threat" no longer conditions military planning in Paris and London. Yet, despite the ostensibly cordial relations among Paris, London, and Bonn, some residual fears continue to color British and French perceptions of the future. Particularly in Paris there is keen appreciation of the political challenge that West Germany's growing economic power poses for France's role in Europe. From the French point of view, one way in which the intrinsic strength of the Federal Republic can be countervailed is through the political credentials derived from a national nuclear panoply. This motivation does not sway British attitudes toward their nuclear forces to the same degree, but there is little question that it at least tinges the outlook from London toward the future evolution of Europe.

French and British Views of the
U.S. Nuclear Pledge

Doubts of the credibility of the American strategic nuclear guarantee for Europe were voiced in Paris long before other European allies openly expressed their concern. They preceded even the transient missile gap in the late fifties. The pivotal event in this respect for the French—and to a somewhat lesser degree for the British—was the Suez Crisis of 1956. The French in particular interpreted U.S. actions in the Suez episode as evidence that the United States, if its vital interests diverged significantly from those of its partners, would abandon its allies and, if necessary, would even act in concert with the Soviet Union. An explicit legacy of the crisis was the conviction in French military and political circles that without a nuclear deterrent of its own, a nation could become abjectly vulnerable to atomic blackmail (Ailleret, 1957; Ely, 1957; Gérardot, 1957).

The launching of Sputnik and the successful Soviet test of an

ICBM in 1957 exacerbated French misgivings and reverberated in London, as well as in other Western European capitals. The emergence of Soviet intercontinental missiles not only cast a deepening shadow on the heretofore unchallenged nuclear supremacy of the United States, but the danger became palpable for the first time that American cities might become hostages to an aggressive strategy of the Soviet Union. The debate in the United States over a "missile gap," particularly in the presidential election in 1960, exacerbated the growing fear in Europe that the nuclear defense of the continent would henceforth be at the mercy of a shifting balance of power.

Charles de Gaulle, after his return to power in 1958, invoked the skepticism of the American nuclear guarantee to develop an explicit rationale that supported France's accelerated quest for independent nuclear capabilities. In so doing, however, he merely gave expression to a broad consensus in French leading circles. At the same time, he reflected the fears elsewhere in Western Europe that remained mostly hidden beneath the larger apprehension that articulation of these fears would precipitate a progressive withdrawal of American power from the continent. President de Gaulle's skepticism was strengthened by his sense of history which suggested that no ally, no matter how sincere his intentions, could remain unflinching in his loyalty over time.

De Gaulle's successors have modified this view, as evidenced in their rapprochement with Britain and their more recent counsel against a premature American disengagement from Western Europe.[5] Yet they have not abandoned the central Gaullist tenet which holds that, irrespective of the state of American-Soviet strategic balance, any American president, no matter how sincerely he may be motivated by alliance obligations, will hesitate to risk the nuclear destruction of the United States in order to save an ally from Soviet clutches. André Fontaine, the well known foreign affairs editor of *Le Monde,* recently articulated this widespread concern in France. He conceded that no American president would turn his back to the U.S. commitment to the North Atlantic alliance. Yet, pointing to growing isolationist tendencies in the United States, Fontaine (1972) predicted that Washington will be less and less inclined to "risk millions of

American lives to preserve any particular part of Western Europe." Fontaine concluded that it was unrealistic to expect the European NATO members to depend indefinitely on the United States for their security.

The British leaders have shared this concern, but have been less willing to voice it. The concern has helped to sustain in successive British governments, including that of Labour leader Wilson, the determination to nurture a British nuclear force in some form or another. Yet, British reticence to discuss officially the possibility of a decoupling of the American strategic force from the defense of Europe relates in good part to the residue of the "special relationship" with the United States. Britain's silence is also related to its investment in a coordinated NATO defense policy that requires the continued involvement of the United States. For British officialdom to question the American nuclear guarantee is tantamount to challenging the cornerstone of Britain's defense policy.

Notwithstanding this silence at the official level, however, there appears to be growing uneasiness in London. The uneasiness is reflected in the shrillness with which British spokesmen argue that basically nothing has changed in the alliance, and that the Nixon Doctrine does not mean a stinting of the American nuclear guarantee, and that American forces will remain encamped in Europe to lend credence to this guarantee. Beneath the official level, there has come a rising volume of doubts. Thus, British strategic thinkers were in the vanguard of those Europeans who early discerned the basic contradictions between U.S.-U.S.S.R. parity at the strategic nuclear level and the threat of U.S. nuclear escalation to deter aggression against Western Europe (see, for example, Martin, 1969).

Anglo-French Views of the Role of Nuclear Weapons

The British were probably the first to recognize the military value of the atom. As early as April 1940, the Maud Committee was established in Britain to explore the feasibility of constructing a uranium bomb. The committee's affirmative findings and its prediction that the destructive power of a nuclear bomb could prove decisive in war triggered the British decision to develop such a weapon. Britain's quest for the atom was sidelined by the more immediate demands of war and was subsequently channeled into cooperative ventures with the United States. Yet there is no question that the early discernment of the atomic bomb as the decisive weapon set the pattern for British military thought in the post-World War II period.[6]

The start of the British atomic program in 1947 was accompanied by a growing body of British military thinking that embraced the supreme deterrent value of nuclear power. Indeed, the conviction in London that Soviet aggression against Western Europe would be deterred essentially by the atomic sword led to the emergence in Great Britain of the massive strategic retaliation concept as early as 1951-1952. Some two to three years before the "new look" became fashionable in Washington, the British had elevated the strategic nuclear bomber to the ultimate expression of military power. The British nuclear bomber squadrons have long since yielded their strategic missions to the Polaris force. Yet the fundamental tenet of the massive strategic retaliation doctrine continues to color much of British strategic thinking.

Like the British, the French had long been engaged in nuclear research. Unlike the British, however, the French had to halt their efforts during World War II. Not until the early fifties did French strategists begin to speculate about the enormous implications of nuclear weapons for modern warfare. Although the French were relative parvenus to the stage of atomic strategy, they managed to grasp much earlier than most others, including the small band of strategic writers in the United States, the political potential derived from ownership of nuclear weaponry. It was this early recognition of the political value as well as the military utility of nuclear weapons that served as the main prod to the French nuclear program.

Reflecting upon the experience in World War II, French military writers discerned in the evolution of twentieth century warfare the progressive dominance of firepower on the battlefield. In war fighting, atomic weapons obviously loomed superior to conventional arms for destroying large military targets or for striking against a massive ground invasion.[7] The recognition in France of the strategic role of nuclear weapons as the instrument of retaliation against the enemy's homeland came apace. Here too, the French perception represented an extension of the wartime experience, particularly of the role of strategic bombing in World War II, and it coincided with the American shift to a strategy of massive retaliation. Yet, as has been suggested, the French were among the first in Europe to understand the psychological dimensions of deterrence and to embrace the conviction that nuclear weapons, in order to dissuade a potential aggressor, need not be addressed solely to defined military targets. Instead, the French believed, the psychological value of nuclear weapons inhered in their awesomeness and in the ambiguity of their use. As the debate in France over the desirability of a French nuclear arsenal gathered momentum in the early fifties, French experts argued that nuclear force meant political leverage as the symbol of great power status and international prestige (see Kelly, 1960).

This concept both spurred and shaped the direction of the French nuclear weapons program under President de Gaulle, who carried the argument to its logical conclusion. Nuclear weapons, contended de Gaulle, represented more than instruments of twentieth century deterrence and defense; as the ultimate weapon, they represented ultimate power and the accreditation of that power on the international stage.

British and French Perceptions of National Nuclear Forces

These early concepts in Paris and later in London regarding the military and political utility of nuclear weapons provided the broad rationales for the development of British and French national nuclear forces beneath what was then regarded as a reliable American protective umbrella. In addition, prognosticators in both Britain and France recognized that the manufacture of military nuclear hardware would yield benefits for the development of peaceful atomic energy and for the general scientific and technological bases of the given country. Indeed, from the beginning of their respective ventures into the nuclear realm, British and French leaders maintained that the industrial and commercial sectors would ultimately reap the benefits of nuclear military research. During Anglo-American collaboration in World War II and when the Attlee government embarked on a British nuclear program after the war, the perceived implications for Britain's industrial future were in the forefront of British nuclear ambitions (Williams, 1961: 119). Meanwhile in France, spokesmen argued that without a nuclear weapons program their nation would be not only a second-rate military and political power, but would be relegated to permanent inferiority in the industrial race as well.[8]

These notions of the collateral values of nuclear power have abided and sustained the rationales behind British and French nuclear programs. There are, however, significant nuances in these rationales that reflect differences in national experience and requirements.

The British Rationale. The justifications advanced in the United Kingdom for the development of national nuclear forces have varied over time. Perhaps no single argument has dominated. Yet, the thrust of such justifications does yield some clues regarding future trends.

Having participated in the joint allied atomic project during the second World War, Britain, as a victorious great power, more or less, took it for granted that this latest weapon had to be part of its armory. Something of this spirit—that if one can have nuclear weapons, one might as well possess them—still persists in Britain. Closely related is the assumption, most fully articulated in the early fifties when British strategists formulated their own doctrine of massive retaliation, that atomic weapons promised a cheaper solution to warfare. The logic of this last assumption does not necessarily point to national nuclear forces, if a fully reliable nuclear ally were available. It is obvious, however, that the British nuclear forces have constituted in part a tacit insurance policy against the collapse of the alliance. In the early fifties, the Churchill government argued that the British nuclear force would supplement the U.S. force by giving priority to those targets that were of vital interest to Britain (Pierre, 1972: 92-93). After the Suez crisis, the Defense White Paper of 1957 drafted by Duncan Sandys (1957: 3), as well as its successor in 1958, laid particular stress on the need for protection against the day when American and British policies might diverge as they had in 1956. This rationale has never been disavowed. Even the Labour Party, when it came into power in 1964, conveniently ignored its earlier campaign rhetoric to the effect that Britain's nuclear force was neither independent nor credible.

Paradoxically, while Britain's nuclear capability serves as a hedge against U.S. nuclear desertion, it has also been seen in the United Kingdom as an instrument to strengthen Anglo-American relations. Before the 1958 U.S.-U.K. agreement for nuclear sharing, Britain's nuclear quest was aimed at least in part toward a restoration of the close Anglo-American partnership of the World War II years; after the 1958 agreement, the preservation of that special relationship remained a strong prop of British nuclear ambitions. Except for some vociferous left-wing and pacifist factions, political and military leaders in London are convinced that nuclear capabilities yield to Britain a degree of political leverage not available to nonnuclear powers.

These national motivations, however, have not inhibited Britain's acceptance of NATO doctrine and targeting. The British Polaris fleet continues, of course, to be guided by national targeting plans in order to project an independent deterrent capability vis-à-vis the Soviet Union. But the submarines are also committed to NATO and to SACEUR's (Supreme Allied Commander/Europe) targeting plans. The British nuclear bomber fleet, moreover, is fully integrated with the NATO forces in a tactical support role as its primary mission. Thus, unlike the French, the British have used their nuclear capability not only to enhance their independence, but also as an instrument to promote the concerted NATO defense effort. Their willingness to operate their nuclear forces within the NATO framework has given the British, at the same time, levers of influence over NATO strategy and planning.

The French Rationale. Already long before General de Gaulle returned to power, French spokesmen of various political persuasions argued that national control lent credibility to nuclear forces. Where the survival of France was concerned, they felt that even a modest nuclear force in the hands of France would be more credible in Soviet eyes than America's powerful threat of nuclear retaliation. In the agressor's calculus of risks versus gains, French strategists reasoned, the nuclear power available to the victim of aggression did not need to be equal to that controlled by the aggressor. If France possessed the capabilities to deliver nuclear strikes against a number of Soviet cities, the Soviet planner would have to consider whether the conquest of French territory would be worth the destruction of these cities. This was called the doctrine of proportional deterrence, with which particularly General Pierre Gallois became identified by English-speaking audiences (see, for example, Gallois, 1961).

The existence of national nuclear forces under separate national commands would bring with it, in French views, the advantage of compounding the uncertainties for the potential aggressor. Thus, the development of French nuclear forces would enhance the overall Western deterrent.

The French belief in the credibility of national nuclear forces is closely related to the concept of the indivisibility of nuclear power. A fundamental tenet of General de Gaulle's credo was that—projects of European economic integration and political cooperation notwithstanding—history was not yet witnessing the demise of the nation-state. National sovereignty remained the supreme expression of power and, hence, inherently indivisible. The control of nuclear force as the most sensitive nerve of that sovereignty was equally indivisible. Hence, de Gaulle looked askance at the various schemes that U.S. officials suggested in their search for a solution to the nuclear sharing problem of the alliance: from the Norstad Plan of 1958 to the Multilateral Force (MLF) proposal of the sixties. The General did not ask the United States to share its command over its own nuclear panoply; but by the same token, he rejected out of hand any scheme that threatened to impinge upon France's exclusive grasp over its national nuclear forces. The concept of indivisibility remains paramount in French nuclear doctrine. As Defense Minister Michel Debré (1971: 397) has reminded American audiences: "The nuclear risk is not indivisible. . . . The decision to employ nuclear forces can be made only by a single nation."

If strategic considerations loomed large in France's nuclear aspirations, political factors played an equally important role. France's nuclear efforts were essentially directed at four political objectives. A first objective involved the enhancement of France's political stature. Not unlike the British, the French were convinced that a ranking member of the world community required nuclear credentials.

A second political goal of France's nuclear efforts was parity with Britain relative to the United States. In the light of centuries of Anglo-French competition, it is not surprising that matching the power and stature of its traditional rival in Europe loomed as a minimum target of France's endeavors. This incentive was magnified in postwar years by French resentment of the privileged place that the United States accorded Britain at the tables of the alliance. The most tangible symbol of Anglo-American amity has been the so-called special relationship in nuclear matters. French resentment of this relationship was by no means limited to the Gaullist milieu; it pervaded political and military circles of every persuasion. Indeed, a major event in the evolution of French policy was the Nassau Agreement between Britain and the United States in 1962. The French discerned in the agreement not only convincing evidence of America's intent to perpetuate its domination over the NATO partners, but also Britain's basic decision to place its special relationship with the United States above the objectives of European cooperation. In the immediate wake of Nassau came General de Gaulle's veto of Britain's entry into the European Common Market, a decision that was loudly applauded in France by Gaullists and anti-Gaullists alike. Although the Pompidou regime has accepted Britain's membership in the Common Market without requiring the dissolution of the Anglo-American special relationship, the latter lingers as a prominent obstacle in Anglo-French relations.

A third political objective of France's nuclear program, again similar to that of the British, was to bolster the nation's role in shaping Europe's future. The French have tended to see themselves as the nation best suited to speak for the continental NATO nations, particularly vis-à-vis the East. Implicit in this notion is the conviction that the Soviets respect nuclear power and know that, by dint of that power, France cannot be cowed into concessions.

Finally, France's nuclear force was intended as a club over Germany. West Germany's place in French threat perceptions and the role of French nuclear weapons as countervailing power against German economic and political strength were mentioned earlier. Beyond these preemptive French aims vis-à-vis Bonn, however, there have loomed some positive objectives as well. A major target of postwar French policies in Europe has been that of tying the Federal Republic of Germany (F.R.G.) as securely as possible to Western moorings in order to prevent any new German adventurism, be it a concerted West German drive for reunification or an attempt in Bonn to play a new balance-of-power game between East and West. From a vantage point in Paris, French nuclear capabilities clearly constitute such moorings. This objective helps to explain General de Gaulle's ardent efforts to level the historic barriers between France and Germany. After Adenauer's departure, the French-German rapprochement cooled perceptibly. The postwar relations between the two countries sank to a nadir when Chancellor Ludwig Erhard, pressed by American MLF diplomacy in effect to exercise a choice between Paris and Washington, opted in favor of the latter. The relations between Paris and Bonn have warmed in the wake of de Gaulle's departure, but they continue to be marred by economic rivalry, fiscal disputes, and competition in the eastern policies of the two countries. The extent to which hopes of a French nuclear hold on West Germany still animate the Pompidou government is difficult to discern. Yet, there are telltale signs. Thus, growing French apprehensions over a withdrawal of American forces from West Germany appear to reflect, at least in part, the notion that the maintenance of American leverage in Bonn may, in fact, be preferable to the contingency of a West Germany left to its own devices.

Beyond the dictates of grand strategy and international politics, France's nuclear program was clearly aimed at domestic requirements as well. General de Gaulle recognized sharply that France's armed forces, whose morale had been shattered by defeat in Indochina and Algeria, needed to be reimbued with a new sense of patriotic pride and élan. The glitter of nuclear weaponry obviously served this objective. Similarly, one of the major factors that animated the French development of a new tactical nuclear missile, the Pluton, has been the need to boost the flagging spirits of the French army, which has suffered in the shadow of the air force and navy—the services entrusted with the strategic nuclear mission.

In short, a broad spectrum of incentives has created and prodded the development of the French *force de dissuasion*. Not every one of these incentives and justifications has found a positive echo among all French political and military circles. Nor is there a real consensus among the political and military leaders. The French Communist Party has consistently opposed the establishment of a national nuclear capability. But in other political sectors—the conservatives, center groups, and most of the noncommunist left—France's nuclear forces are, if not strongly supported, at least accepted as a fact of national life. This acceptance militates against any French readiness in the near future to share the reins over the national nuclear forces. Whether it may permit nuclear cooperation or coordination beneath the pinnacles of decision-making and command and control remains to be seen.

Anglo-French Strategic Preferences

The strategic views of the British and the French are a blend of their perceptions of the threat, of the credibility of the American nuclear guarantee, and of the role of nuclear weapons. These strategic concepts have also been conditioned in large measure by their respective national experience and the limitations of military capabilities. Thus, the overwhelming emphasis on the countervalue mission that both Paris and London assign to their respective strategic forces mirrors above all the fact that neither country possesses the requisite numbers of weapons with the necessary refinements to provide its forces with a counterforce role.

The British insist on retaining national control over their nuclear forces in order to have in reserve national means to cope with international emergencies. At the same time, however, the British are loyal to the principle of the integrated allied defense structure and have committed their nuclear forces to NATO in wartime. Great Britain, moreover, has officially endorsed NATO's flexible response strategy, but only insofar as this implies a strictly limited phase of conventional defense. Few British strategists believe that the make-up of Western defenses will grant much in the way of flexibility in the event of war.[9]

More important, perhaps, the British do not want alliance planning to be keyed to an extended period of conventional defense for fear of the destruction it would wreak upon Western Europe. Conservative and Labour leaders alike clearly prefer a deterrent strategy anchored primarily in the threat of strategic retaliation. This view is probably not shared by many of Britain's military commanders who appreciate the requirements of defending Western Europe on the ground and would be prepared to use tactical nuclear weapons in a militarily effective fashion.[10] But in political circles, the prevalent view is to reject a sustained conventional defense and to regard the use of tactical nuclear weapons as a penultimate resort—one that is preferable to immediate recourse to catastrophic strategic strikes, but at the same time does not promise very much in the way of avoiding disaster.

True, Britain no longer adheres to the strategy of instant massive retaliation in its pristine form. Yet the desire for a low nuclear threshold combined with the efforts to limit the range of NATO options suggests that there is little "flexibility" in the British interpretation of flexible response. Residue of the massive retaliation era can be seen in Britain's countervalue strategy for its Polaris forces if used in a national role. The high priority Britain accords to keeping Moscow within its national targeting array, as reflected by its efforts to improve the penetration capability of the Polaris missiles (Smart, 1971: 12), is reminiscent of Britain's original belief in the psychological value of strategic bombing.

French strategic thinking has several elements in common with the concepts voiced in London. Until recently, the prevailing French view of conventional ground forces—their own *forces de manoeuvre* [11] as well as NATO forces—has hewed to a tripwire concept, which assigned to forces in the field the function of triggering the threat of a strategic nuclear response. This view accorded with the French concern to prevent a protracted conventional conflict, one that possibly would spill into France. It also was consistent with their low estimate of a Soviet intention to launch a deliberate massive invasion—an assumption that was central to General de Gaulle's decision to withdraw French forces from the integrated NATO commands in 1966. Like the British, the French gave priority to deterrence over defense and pressed for a low nuclear threshold and the early use of nuclear weapons in NATO strategy. American efforts in the sixties to impose a strategy of flexible response with its emphasis on a conventional defense stirred strong opposition in Paris and were a factor in France's decision to withdraw from NATO's military command structure.

Until recently, official French military thinking deliberately downplayed the role of tactical nuclear weapons. General Charles Ailleret (1964), the late French Chief of Staff of the Armed Forces, was the major exponent of those who rejected the use of tactical nuclear weapons. Other key officials, however, have stressed the military mission of tactical nuclear weapons in halting an enemy thrust. The controversy over tactical weapons was triggered in the interservice debate that surfaced in the years 1964-1965. A group of ranking army officers, led by the then Chief of Staff, General Louis le Puloch (1964), argued that an army needed to have tactical nuclear weapons at its disposal to attack the advance elements of an invading enemy. These officers also questioned the effectiveness of the Mirage IV bombers, France's only nuclear delivery systems at the time.[12] The air force, led by its chief, General André Martin (1964), rebutted this contention with the argument that the way to attack an enemy was to strike him in the rear, preferably in his own territory. Although the controversy continued, the government's decision to equip both the army and air force with tactical nuclear weapons helped to allay the rivalry between the services.

The March 1969 speech by General Michel Fourquet (1969), Ailleret's successor, manifested the evolution in French military thinking since 1964-1965. It signaled a major change in French strategic doctrine and it came close to a French version of the flexible response strategy in which not only the strategic nuclear forces, but also the conventional and tactical nuclear forces were to play a critical role.

Fourquet believed that a conventional attack should be met with conventional forces. When necessary, however, France should be prepared to resort to tactical nuclear weapons in order to demonstrate its resolve and to test the enemy's intentions. Fourquet made clear that the use of the tactical weapons was not meant to be symbolic—thus denying the demonstrative option preferred by the British—but had rather to satisfy the requirements of maximum effectiveness. He did not spell out specific employment options, although other French writers have stressed the *offensive* use of tactical nuclear weapons. Fourquet joined previous French spokesmen in contending that the threshold at which the tactical nuclear weapons were to be launched could not be fixed in advance, and that the specific contingency use would remain the prerogative of the French government. As in the case of French doctrine for strategic nuclear forces, timing and conditions for the use of the tactical weapons were to be kept deliberately ambiguous. Generally, however, Fourquet suggested a relatively early resort to tactical nuclear weapons—indeed, earlier than NATO, which he feared might lack the firmness to halt an invasion of West Germany. In Fourquet's view, the use of the tactical atomic weapons hopefully would obviate a strategic nuclear exchange; in any case, tactical nuclear weapons would strengthen the credibility of the strategic nuclear deterrent.

Fourquet thus became one of the first ranking officials to posit in some detail the relationship between the strategic nuclear, tactical nuclear, and conventional forces, and their assigned missions. Other French spokesmen have elaborated on

Fourquet's notions. Thus Michel Debré (1972c: 17), while placing a deterrent label on tactical nuclear weapons, officially affirmed the counterforce role of these weapons in defense.

The dialogue by prominent French analysts on the role of tactical nuclear weapons reveals how much more flexible French strategic thinking has become since the days when the simple notion of instant strategic retaliation seemed to blanket military thinking in Paris. The change in French strategy reflected France's broadening spectrum of military capabilities. The French are now more disposed to ponder the "unthinkable" and to contemplate the mechanics and nuances of a viable defense of Western Europe. Contrary to the wistful expectations in neighboring countries, however, this broader strategic view of the common defense does not presage a French return to a full embrace of alliance planning. French forces will remain under undiluted French control. In General de Gaulle's inimitable imagery, "France must keep her personality, her figure, her soul."

France's insistence on retaining undiluted control over its nuclear forces and its corresponding strategic concepts virtually preclude its return to the integrated NATO fold. It also augurs ill for the possibility of Anglo-French nuclear collaboration beyond some technical data sharing and a limited degree of operational coordination.

In Britain, two trends of thought are salient. Labour leaders are clearly unwilling to consider Anglo-French nuclear cooperation—let alone such cooperation outside a NATO framework. This view is tinged with ideological antipathy toward Gaullism, but it also reflects the fear of a premature disengagement of the United States from the defense of Western Europe. The Conservative position is somewhat more flexible and has room for European nuclear efforts "complementary" to NATO. In his 1967 Godkin lectures at Harvard, Edward Heath (1970: 73) spoke of pooling British and French nuclear forces and holding them in trust for Europe. A similar thrust emerged in a 1970 study by the Bow Group (Griffiths and Niblock, 1970: 13), a semi-official Conservative research group, which favored the development of a "European controlled deterrent." This does not mean that the Conservatives are eager to rush into an Anglo-

French nuclear partnership. The British face the dilemma of how to engineer cooperative defense projects in Europe, and particularly nuclear projects, without alienating the United States and sacrificing the trans-Atlantic nuclear links that underwrite European security and materially assist Britain in its own nuclear program. This is clearly the reason why, their earlier enthusiasm notwithstanding, the Conservatives since their return to office have demonstrated little haste in promoting Anglo-French nuclear collaboration.

In short, the concern in London and Paris about the declining credibility of the U.S. nuclear guarantee appears to be the major strategic reason for the British and French to combine their nuclear muscles. There are, however, other factors in the policy equations of both countries. For example, what about economic and technological incentives? Would they be likely to promote a nuclear marriage between London and Paris?

Technological Considerations

The histories of both the French and British nuclear programs are relatively long. Thus, the genesis of French nuclear force was in the first decade of the Fourth Republic. Successive governments and national assemblies in the Fourth Republic were prepared to nurture the effort by allocating the necessary funds and technical resources to create the infrastructure for the French nuclear program, which in February 1960 led to the first French nuclear explosion at the Reggane test site in the Sahara.[13]

The British nuclear program antedates that of the French. Indeed, the United Kingdom was a pioneer on the atomic road with its initial efforts in 1941—efforts that were subsequently joined with those of the United States in the fruitful Manhattan Project. This early start and the benefits of their wartime collaboration with the United States gave the British the necessary research, development, and production base for their own nuclear program after the United States terminated Anglo-American nuclear cooperation shortly following the war. The solidity of this base was demonstrated in October 1952, when the first British atomic device was detonated. Five years later the British staged their first successful thermonuclear explosion test.

Current French Nuclear Forces

The French military program law for the years 1960-1964 called for a nuclear force of Mirage IV aircraft armed with nuclear bombs. This law also authorized initial funding for the first nuclear-powered missile-launching submarine, the development of strategic missiles, and the construction of the Pierrelatte isotope separation plant. Under the second program law for 1965-1970, the Mirage IV force was completed, the second generation of France's nuclear force consisting of surface-to-surface ballistic missiles was begun, and construction of two additional submarines was commissioned. Research and development of thermonuclear warheads, a submarine ballistic missiles system, and tactical nuclear weapons were also authorized. The third program law covering the period 1971-1975 continued the development of submarine ballistic missiles and thermonuclear warheads, which formed the third generation of French nuclear weapons. The third law also specified production guidelines for the construction of additional submarines and tactical nuclear weapons.

The French inventory of Mirage bombers, originally projected to include 62 aircraft, now consists of some 57 bombers. The planes are organized into two wings, which in turn are divided into nine squadrons. The squadrons are dispersed over nine airfields, all of them relatively remote from large cities. Of these 57 aircraft, 36 are deployed at all times. Each is armed with a 70 kiloton fission bomb. The remainder serve in air-defensive, training, or reserve missions or are in maintenance (Kohl, 1971: 180-181). According to the third military program law, the Mirage IV force is projected to remain operational at least until 1976 (Kolodziej, 1972: 1092-1093).

The Mirage bomber force is supported by a fleet of 12 KC-135 tanker planes that were purchased from the United States in 1962. Refueled over the Baltic or the North Sea, the bomber force would be capable of reaching targets to the west of a longitudinal line running through Moscow. Refueling requirements, however, place a serious limitation on the French strategic bomber force.

The second French nuclear system to reach operational capability was that of a surface-to-surface missile. Two complexes of nine missiles each are now deployed in hardened underground silos in the Albion Plateau in southeastern France; the positioning of nine additional missiles has been postponed until they can be fitted with thermonuclear warheads. The French IRBMs are two-stage missiles with 150 kiloton warheads (Brown, 1972: 65).

The projected "punch" of France's nuclear power, however, resides in its missile-armed submarine force. Present plans call for five nuclear-powered missile-launching submarines. Each is to carry 16 SLBMs that can deliver 500 kiloton warheads over a range of 1,200-1,300 nautical miles. The first ship, *Le Redoutable,* is operational; a second vessel has also been launched. The third should be operational by 1974, to be followed by the remaining two before 1980 (France, 1972: 12).

The French nuclear inventory has been expanded to include tactical as well as strategic weapons. The second military program law provided for the development of a tactical nuclear warhead suitable for delivery by either aircraft or ground missiles. Current French fighter-bombers, including the Mirage III-E, Mystère IV-A, F 100-D, and Etendard IV-N, as well as the interceptor Vautour II-N, are capable of delivering tactical nuclear bombs. These aircraft total 17 squadrons assigned to the Naval Air Force, the Air Defense Command, and the Tactical Air Force. Many of the current aircraft entered the inventory in the early 1960s, but there are plans to replace them. The Mirage III-E and the planned Dassault F-1, an interceptor and ground attack aircraft, will be able to fire air-to-surface nuclear missiles.

The French are also developing a tactical surface-to-surface nuclear missile, the Pluton, for deployment with the five mechanized divisions of the French army. The missile, with a range of up to 75 nautical miles, will be mounted on tracked carriers and can carry a 10 to 15 kiloton warhead (Brown, 1972: 68). According to reports (Le Monde, 1971a), the warhead for the Pluton was completed in 1971. It is expected that by 1975 both the French ground forces and tactical aircraft will be armed with the missile.

Current British Nuclear Forces

Consistent with its strategic predilections, Britain in its nuclear program has emphasized primarily the development of long-range forces. Except for its nuclear strike aircraft, which since 1969 have been given a tactical support role, Britain has not developed tactical nuclear forces, but has relied on U.S. systems. Even the V-bomber force was originally conceived as a strategic force. Furthermore, unlike the French, the British do not have any land-based nuclear missiles. Efforts to develop the Blue Streak, an intermediate range surface-to-surface ballistic missile, failed when mounting costs and the recognition of impending obsolescence forced the British in April 1960 to cancel that program.

Great Britain today possesses four Polaris-type submarines, each armed with sixteen A-3 missiles. The approximately 2,500 nautical mile range of the Polaris missiles is sufficient to reach all major cities in the western Soviet Union. Each missile carries three reentry vehicles, which are armed with thermonuclear warheads of approximately 200 kilotons but which are not independently targeted (Blackman, 1972: 341). Plans for a fifth nuclear submarine were canceled in 1965 by the Labour government, partly in response to economic pressures and partly in deference to the party's prior campaign rhetoric about abandoning the British nuclear deterrent.

The operational patterns guiding the ballistic submarines of France and Britain are similar. Both nations have adopted the manning model of the U.S. Polaris submarine. Thus, each British submarine is operated by two crews in order to maximize the time of the vessel on operating stations. Each submarine carries out four patrols a year of about 60 days. Both Britain and France have designed their nuclear propulsion reactors for three years of sustained operations. The British had originally estimated that replacement of the nuclear propulsion cores would require about six months; the first overhaul experience showed, however, that nearly a year was required. Hence, only one British submarine will be on station at all times. It is possible, however, that the experience gained in the first refit can reduce the overhaul periods (Smart, 1971: 4, 15).

British nuclear strike aircraft include its 8 Vulcan bomber squadrons, 55 Canberra light bombers and Buccaneer attack aircraft, some 20 F-4 Phantoms, and some Harriers, Britain's first V'STOL fighter-bombers.

Unlike the French, the British have not tried to develop a tactical surface-to-surface nuclear missile, choosing to rely instead on their aircraft and on the Honest John rocket launchers and eight-inch Howitzers supplied by the United States for use with American nuclear warheads (Cliffe, 1972: 35).

Technical Assets and Shortcomings

An examination of the comparative technical assets and shortcomings in the French and British nuclear programs suggests that France would receive relatively greater benefits in an exchange of know-how and experience with Great Britain. Because the United States was willing to underwrite Britain's nuclear plans, the United Kingdom has reached, in many aspects, a much more sophisticated level of technology and delivery systems design than France. To be sure, the necessity of going it alone has yielded several important independent assets for French strategic forces that would otherwise not have redounded had France relied on the nuclear tutelage of the United States. But France's nuclear forces were developed at much greater costs in resources and time than those of Britain. Moreover, because of its late start, France's nuclear technology and its technology for supporting systems still lag behind those of Britain.

A salient asset derived by France from its go-it-alone policy is its ability to manage the many and varied tasks associated with the research and development of nuclear weapons. The French development of ballistic missiles was begun in 1958. In the following year, the government formed SEREB *(Société pour l'étude et réalisation d'engins balistiques),* an organization designed to manage the missile effort that gradually succeeded in enlisting almost every sector of the French aerospace industry. Coordinated by SEREB, the French production capacity for propellants and missiles is, according to some observers, probably the most advanced in the world beyond those of the United States and the Soviet Union (Smart, 1971: 11).

In the production of nuclear materials as well, France appears to have the advantage over Britain. France has a considerable technical capability in its Pierrelatte facility, which produces the highly enriched uranium needed for nuclear submarine propulsion reactors and thermonuclear weapons; Pierrelatte is also the site of the French uranium hexafluoride ("hex") gas conversion plant, which supplies hex for the uranium enrichment process. Pierrelatte can produce sufficient highly enriched uranium for France's forseeable weapons requirements.

The same is true of France's plutonium production. France has two specialized plutonium production reactors at Marcoule, as well as chemical reprocessing plants at Marcoule and La Hague. The total production capacity of weapons grade plutonium can cover French needs. France produces annually some 1,200 metric tons of natural uranium, from which either enriched uranium or plutonium can be derived. If its exploitation of African resources is included, France has access to proven uranium reserves of over 100,000 tons. Deuterium and lithium, necessary for fusion reactions, are easily obtainable by France. Finally, France has two reactors at Marcoule for tritium production, even though the process is extremely expensive (Smart, 1971: 9-10).

Britain, on the other hand, is not producing any critical material for its weapon program. Britain's existing requirements are met from an existing stockpile of tritium and by trade or purchase of enriched uranium from the United States. The gaseous diffusion plant at Capehurst is presently used for Britain's commercial atomic energy program; it has not produced enriched uranium for weapon use since 1962 (Smart, 1971: 9). Neither does Britain produce any weapons grade plutonium. The plutonium production reactors were shut down as a result of a major accident and have never been reactivated because of economic considerations. Britain's current plutonium production is now a by-product of its electrical industry and fully committed to the expansion of its electrical power base. For uranium ore Britain depends on Canada, which has a large production capacity. Access to this resource is assured.

In short, Britain's enriched uranium capacity as well as other critical material production is used for satisfying its commercial power requirements. Barring a major reversal of policy, Britain will not have the critical material resources necessary to support a significant expansion of its nuclear weapons stockpile. It would be dependent on external sources.

Part of France's infrastructure to support its nuclear weapons program are its facilities for the flight testing of missiles and for the testing of nuclear devices and warheads. The Landes Test Center, completed in 1966, is designed for flight testing of strategic missiles. A French-Portuguese agreement for a station on an island in the Azores permits the tracking of missiles launched from the Landes Test Center. France also maintains a test flight launch facility on the Ile de Levant in the Mediterranean. In 1967, France completed the large nuclear test center in French Polynesia in the Pacific, where two atolls are used for atmospheric testing (Kohl, 1971: 186-188). Realizing that it would need to continue testing in the atmosphere, France never signed the Limited Test Ban Treaty of 1963, but kept its option open. The series of tests in the summer of 1972 indicate France's continued requirement for such tests.

By contrast, Great Britain in its testing requirements relies almost completely on the United States. As a signatory to the Partial Test Ban Treaty, Britain no longer conducts atmospheric tests. Instead, Britain since 1963 has used U.S. underground facilities for nuclear explosions (Smart, 1971: 11). Britain also has access to the facilities of the Woomera missile test range in Australia and to the U.S. Atlantic test range for flight testing of the Polaris missile.

While France's independent venture into the nuclear field has reaped assets of indigenous strength, it has also drawn penalties. Particular weaknesses of France's nuclear program are in the areas of nuclear warhead design and supporting systems technology.

By far the greatest such shortcoming in the development of the French nuclear force to date has been the difficulty in designing and producing a compact thermonuclear warhead with high yield-to-weight ratio that would be suitable for missile delivery. Moreover, the development of a light-weight thermonuclear warhead is needed in order to produce a more flexible tactical warhead for the land-based and air-delivered systems. France at one time expected to arm by 1970 both its land- and sea-based missiles with thermonuclear warheads; now these are not expected to be available for operational deployment until 1976 (France, 1972: 13). Britain, on the other hand, tested its first thermonuclear device as early as 1957. British thermonuclear warheads are operational and deployed in the Blue Steel and Polaris missiles and in free-falling bombs.

Problems encountered by the French in warhead design, moreover, have victimized other areas of nuclear modernization. The alternatives that France faced at an early state of its nuclear program were (a) to focus efforts primarily on the creation of an operational thermonuclear warhead, or (b) to allocate part of its resources and efforts to designing other advanced techniques for its nuclear forces, such as hardening, penetration aids, and multiple reentry vehicles (MRVs). Since the development of suitable warheads constitutes the most critical requirement for its nuclear program, France concentrated on the first alternative. As a result of this choice, France's technology for penetration aids and MRVs is still considerably behind that of Britain, which enjoyed U.S. support in these areas.

French industry, moreover, has not yet been able to produce the powerful sophisticated computers essential for the complicated calculations in the design of nuclear warheads and missiles. The British would be in a position to assist the French in this area.

France has also encountered problems in the development of its nuclear-armed submarines and accompanying missile system. The French began the construction of the first nuclear submarine as early as 1958 in the expectation that unenriched uranium could serve as fuel for the propulsion reactor. Within about a year, however, this plan proved to be infeasible. France then, in May 1959, was able to reach an agreement with the United States for the supply of highly enriched uranium, a more appropriate fuel for a submarine reactor. The uranium supplied by the United States enabled the French to test a land-based prototype propulsion reactor. The French promptly undertook a series of studies of submarine reactor systems, but not until March 1964 did they lay the keel of the *Redoutable,* the first French nuclear armed submarine. The British began construction of their first nuclear armed submarine at about the same time. But, whereas the British deployed their first submarine in 1967, the French vessel did not become operational until 1971. To be sure, Britain had received substantial U.S. technological support and material for nuclear propulsion systems since 1958 and for its Polaris program since the 1962 Nassau Agreement. Moreover, France was undoubtedly plagued by financial problems, while Britain acquired the Polaris systems with only very modest research and development expenses. Nevertheless, inexperience with nuclear powered submarines and lack of technological expertise also contributed to the much longer lead times for the French.

In addition to the difficulties in the field of nuclear propulsion, the French had to solve the problems connected with the ejection of a missile from a submerged submarine and ignition of the engines once the missile would be airborne (Smart, 1971: 11). The deployment of the *Redoutable* suggests that some of these problems have been overcome. As in the area of nuclear propulsion, Britain has considerable experience in the underwater firing of missiles.

Furthermore, unlike the British, the French have not yet been able to solve the problems associated with lengthening the range of their missiles. The relatively short range of the French seaborne missiles—some 1,200 to 1,300 miles—restricts the area from which an attack could be launched against Soviet targets, thus increasing the vulnerability of French submarines to Soviet antisubmarine warfare.

There is another area related to the nuclear submarines in which the French are at a significant disadvantage compared to the British. Even though sensitive nuclear technology is generally not involved, the French have serious problems with recruiting and training nuclear submarine crews. The British, with their four Polaris ships operational for some years and their training in the United States, have much more experience than the French and have mastered many of the problems that confronted them in the early years.

In brief, a comparison of the strengths and weaknesses in the French and British nuclear programs suggests that at this stage the French would stand to gain the most in an Anglo-French

⌐arrangement for sharing technology and expertise. The British
could provide the French valuable assistance in thermonuclear
warhead technology and in almost every area related to the
construction and operation of the strategic nuclear submarines
and accompanying armament. The French could offer the British
their expertise in the design and production of missiles, their
testing facilities, and some of the critical materials for nuclear
systems. But in each of these areas the British have been able to
use more advanced U.S. data and testing sites. At this point the
French have not yet reached in their nuclear development the
level of expertise the British obtained from the United States.
From a vantage point in London, the asymmetry in the level of
the British and French nuclear programs argues agsinst Anglo-
French nuclear sharing. The British, moreover, are committed not
to transfer any of their American-received nuclear data to another
party, and the development of their nuclear forces has depended
so heavily on the United States that it would be extremely
difficult to determine what constitutes U.S., what British,
technology.

True, the availability of nuclear and nuclear-related data led
the British, partly in response to economic pressures, to deem-
phasize their own indigenous research and development effort. It
appears reasonable to expect that the more vital French nuclear
establishment will gradually overtake the British technological
lead. Meanwhile, however, the very dependence of the British on
the United States in supporting their present nuclear capability
and possibly the potential improvement of this capability is likely
to sponsor extreme caution in London to avoid jeopardizing the
nuclear nexus with Washington. Without explicit U.S. approval
and encouragement, therefore, the British are unlikely to enter
into any kind of Anglo-French combine.

Economic Aspects

Economic incentives that would be entailed in possible Anglo-French nuclear cooperation are overshadowed by political and military considerations. Nevertheless, economic factors are important if only because they impose constraints on the scope and rate of development of the respective nuclear programs. Potential economic savings could be a valid consideration in weighing the benefits of Anglo-French nuclear cooperation. This section, therefore, examines the trends in the defense budgets of Britain and France, especially the portions allocated to nuclear weapons programs, in order to (1) estimate the capabilities of the two countries to sustain economically the kinds of nuclear programs that meet their larger national policy goals, and (2) discern what economic benefits could accrue to each from nuclear cooperation.

British and French Overall Defense Expenditures and Expenditures on Nuclear Forces

Over the years the defense expenditures of Britain and France as percentages of their GNP have steadily declined. In 1971, according to the estimates of the Institute of Strategic Studies (1972: 70), Britain devoted 4.7% of its GNP to defense, France had gone down to 3.1%. The French thus spend relatively less on defense than their British counterparts, although approximately the same part of their total budget is devoted to defense and their defense expenditure per capita is also very close ($109 for Britain, and $101 for France).

In national expenditures for nuclear forces, the patterns in Great Britain and France are quite dissimilar. Although a precise comparison of British and French nuclear expenditures is difficult, partly because the exact costs of their total nuclear programs are not available, Tables 1 and 2 indicate that the French are spending a much larger portion of the national defense budget for nuclear forces than are the British. This disparity in allocations between the two countries is projected to continue. The French will pursue the development of their *force de dissuasion* at a level that seems to absorb a relatively high proportion of their overall defense expenditures. The British nuclear costs are expected to rise only moderately.[14]

The explanation of the marked disparity shown by Tables 1 and 2 resides mainly in two factors: (1) the British began their nuclear program earlier than the French, and had incurred their major costs before 1965; (2) the British profited from the highly advantageous nuclear sharing relationship with the United States

TABLE 1
BRITISH SPENDING ON NUCLEAR FORCES AS PERCENTAGE OF TOTAL DEFENSE BUDGET

Year	Percentage of Defense Budget[a]	ISS Estimates[b]
1965	6.0[c]	9.6[c]
1966	4.8	
1967	4.7	
1968	4.1	
1969	2.6	
1970	1.4	
1971	1.3[c]	3.1[c]
1972	1.3[c] (est.)	
1965-1971	3.6[c]	6.3[c]

a. Great Britain, **Statement on the Defence Estimates** for the stipulated years (London: Her Majesty's Stationery Office).
b. Smart, 1971: 20.
c. The differences between the two sources result from different assumptions on what items should be included in nuclear spending. The defense budget figures include only the actual running cost figures of the four Polaris boats, no R&D expenditures.

TABLE 2
FRENCH SPENDING ON NUCLEAR FORCES AS
PERCENTAGE OF TOTAL DEFENSE BUDGET

Year	ISS Calculations[a]	Le Monde Statements
1965	27.7	
1966		
1967	30.1	25.0[b]
1968		
1969		20.0[b]
1970		17.2[c]
1971	18.6	
1965-1971	25.5	

a. Smart, 1971: 20.
b. **Le Monde**, 1969c.
c. **Le Monde**, 1969b and 1969a.

and spent much less than would have been necessary if, like the French, they had been forced to build their nuclear force without outside assistance. Especially beneficial to the British was the agreement worked out at Nassau in 1962, according to which the United States agreed to sell Polaris missiles (less warheads) to Britain. Even if the British had paid their pro rata share of the research and development costs of the missiles (which should have been 12%, on a ratio of five British to 41 American boats), the Polaris agreement would have been a financial windfall. As it turned out, however, the British acquired their Polaris forces at cut-rate prices. American defense officials had intended to charge the British the pro rata 12% of R&D, but President Kennedy arranged with the British Ambassador that Britain would have to pay only a 5% overcharge on the production price of the A-3 missile as its contribution to the large R&D expenditure by the United States (Pierre, 1972: 242).

Future of Economic Base for Nuclear Forces

The French economy overall is in a better position to bear national defense burdens than is the British. Two decades ago Britain boasted a greater total GNP and per capita GNP, and a greater economic growth rate than France. The situation is now reversed by all three criteria. France boasts one of the fastest growing economies in Europe; during the 1965-1971 period, the French GNP grew at a rate of 5.7%, as contrasted with a rate of 2.2% in Britain (U.S. Agency for International Development, 1972: 5).

France, with a healthier economy, is spending a smaller percentage of its national resources for defense. In 1971, partly because French economic growth is expected to remain high, the French government attempted to stabilize the defense budget at 3.5% of GNP. Nevertheless, competitive priorities between national defense and nonmilitary domestic programs forced the defense portion of GNP down to 3.0% (Le Monde, 1971b).

Even though the British economy is not as robust as that of France, the British spend slightly more of their GNP than do the French on defense, and can no doubt sustain this level. British defense expenditures have, like the French, declined from a higher percentage of GNP in the 1950s (about 10% in 1952) to the current level of less than 5%. The British nuclear budget is such a small fraction (some 3%) of overall defense spending that it could be multiplied without causing a significant rise in the portion of GNP spent for defense. Even were the British to lose the benefits of the nuclear sharing arrangements with the United States in the next few years, the economic impact would not be critical. Britain's nuclear cost curve is in a "valley" between the peak expenditures of acquiring their nuclear force in the 1960s, and the expected future peak of a next generation of nuclear development when the Polaris submarines will near the end of their useful life.

Economic Implications of Nuclear Cooperation

It is possible to infer from the disparate economic patterns of the British and French nuclear programs at least some broad implications concerning the economic advantages or disadvantages of nuclear sharing.

Thanks to their much earlier start and by dint of U.S. assistance, the British may be said to have reached a plateau of nuclear development, while the French are still struggling uphill. It is true that the program objectives of the two nations differ; while British strategic ambitions are invested almost wholly in that country's ballistic missile submarine force, the French deterrent is projected to embrace a triad: bombers, land-based missiles, and submarines. In any event, the British objective, while more limited, has been mainly achieved, while the French have yet some distance to go in the attainment of their basic objectives. At this stage in the comparative development of nuclear capabilities in the two countries, there would seem to be few sharp economic incentives propelling either country toward cooperative ventures in nuclear development and production.

There is no reason to assume that Britain could not sustain its present low level of expenditures for its nuclear forces. Although France devotes a higher funding level to its nuclear program, it can also continue to bear these expenses. France can even increase this portion of its defense budget without causing a rise in defense spending that would jeopardize its economy. If necessary, France could also in response to political pressures stretch out the development of its nuclear capability over a number of years and implement the program within politically acceptable defense budgets.

Anglo-French collaboration in strategic planning or operational questions is conceivable, as is perhaps even the sharing of technology in which each country would pay its own way. Yet it would be awkward for partners to proceed for very long without facing up to the problem that one has to allocate substantially more funds to the program than the other.

As long as the British are able to sustain their nuclear forces at the present low level of spending, the promises of savings would seem to exert little pull on London toward a cooperative arrangement with the French. As far as the future is concerned —and particularly the likely economic requirements that will be imposed by the development of second-generation nuclear systems once the current Polaris force fades into obsolescence—the British can draw comfort from the apparent circumstance that the sluggishness of the British economy is a temporary phenomenon. The hope may seem valid that by the time the new requirements will assert themselves the economy will have recovered sufficiently to shoulder the added burden. From the British vantage point, moreover, the economic equation is not simply one of direct gains and losses entailed in a nuclear relationship with France. If the British compare the economic advantages (whatever they may be) of cooperation with France with the future penalties entailed in an abrogation of the economic sharing arrangement with the United States (assuming that such an abrogation would be risked through a nuclear entente with the French), then the calculus of economic gain versus risk clearly would militate against cooperation with France.

Conversely, the economic incentive for France in nuclear cooperation with Great Britain seems clear. Two major tasks lie ahead for the French: completion of their ballistic missile submarines and the development of sophisticated thermonuclear warheads. In both these realms, the British enjoy design and operational experience that, if made available to France, could save the latter time and money. If the broader spectrum of nuclear weapons technology in both countries is considered, more complicated patterns of relative advantages in expertise on both sides, and attendant economic tradeoffs, emerge. Without delving into these complexities, suffice it to reiterate that in general economic terms France would, at this stage, have more to gain than to lose by entering into a cooperative arrangement with the United Kingdom. If, as part of such a collaborative venture, the United States relaxed its restrictions on nuclear data sharing with France, the advantages for Paris would seem to be all the more promising.

In short, an examination of purely economic incentives (divorced from political and other considerations) in Great Britain and France for nuclear cooperation yields a clear conclusion: the British would tend to see few economic benefits, and probably some economic penalties, in a nuclear sharing arrangement with France. The French, on the other hand, would currently stand to gain from such an arrangement.

The Political Factors Bearing Upon European Nuclear Cooperation: Incentives and Constraints

The previous sections have probed the strategic, technological, and economic parameters of possible Franco-British nuclear cooperation. The importance of these factors notwithstanding, it seems clear that the likelihood of nuclear cooperation in Europe will hinge not merely on strategic, technological, and economic considerations. Rather, should Franco-British nuclear cooperation come about, it will be the consequence of a political decision taken by the two countries—a decision that will be shaped largely by political considerations.

A host of political issues bears upon the problem. The variables derive from a complexity of trends within Western Europe and in the relationships between West European countries with the United States on the one hand, and with the Soviet/Warsaw Pact nations on the other. This discussion focuses on what appear to be the salient issues: (1) British and French attitudes toward European evolution; (2) West German attitudes and policies; (3) Soviet policy; and (4) American policy and legal constraints.

French and British Approach to West European Evolution

Speculation over possible Franco-British nuclear cooperation has been sparked in the past few years primarily by Britain's entry into the European Economic Community. The speculation has been fed by a number of assumptions and expectations that, in simplified form, might be described as follows: (1) the past barriers to Franco-British cooperation have resided in the political estrangement between those two countries as well as in the exaggerated emphasis in both nations on "national sovereignty" prerogatives; (2) the very facts of Britain's entry into the EEC and of the attending Franco-British rapprochement suggest a possible moderation in both countries of these past philosophical barriers to political cooperation.

Yet are these assumptions justified? To be sure, French assent to British entry into the Common Market has reflected in good part the recognition in Paris of a certain compatibility of views in France and Great Britain regarding the ultimate goals of European cooperation. President Pompidou and Prime Minister Heath have agreed that some form of political unity is a major objective of their respective European policies. The French President (Pompidou, 1971: 2) has called upon European nations to "work together to reach a real unity first in the economic field and gradually in all other fields, including, of course, that of politics." Mr. Heath (Pompidou, 1971: 2) has echoed this view: "Europe must grow steadily together in unity and . . . Britain should be a part of that wider community."

It is clear, however, that when President Pompidou and Prime Minister Heath invoke the concept of European "unity," both refer to a process of political cooperation or harmonization in Western Europe that falls considerably short of the ideal advocated by the proponents of European political integration or federation. The emphasis continues to be upon the inviolate nature of the nation-state. Indeed, President Pompidou (1972: 3) justified France's acceptance of Britain into the EEC quite frankly with the argument that the United Kingdom's entry would shore up the national sovereignty principle in the evolution of Western Europe. Thus, he pointed out at a press conference in March 1972:

> To join with a people (the British) which, perhaps more than any other people in the world, is concerned with keeping its national identity, is also to make the choice in favor of a formula for Europe which will conserve the individuality of the nations which compose it.

Prime Minister Heath has obliged by spelling out a prescription for unity that stresses a careful and gradual approach to the phenomenon, and an ultimate objective that resembles, albeit in less detailed form, the "confederal" model of Western Europe held aloft by President de Gaulle and his successors. He has warned (1969: 42) against "short cuts," clearly referring to supranational experiments:

> The unity of Europe will in the end be achieved by European governments forming the habit of working together. . . . Confidence between governments is the only lasting cement for the unity of Europe. The underlying analysis of M. Monnet and the other founding fathers of the Communities was that the government of the Six would begin by working together for the abolition of tariffs and the creation of a common market. . . . They would gradually extend the range of their cooperation until it passed beyond purely economic matters into foreign policy and defense. . . . I am sure that this still remains the only realistic approach to European unity, and that short cuts can only lead to a further round of disappointments which neither Britain nor Europe can afford.

Thus, in the light of the available evidence, the French-British political rapprochement emerges as neither the consequence nor the precursor of fundamentally changing attitudes in Paris or London toward Western European political unification. The carefully coached approbation that President Pompidou gave the European unity goal at the EEC summit meeting in October 1972 by no means signaled a change in basic French attitudes. While the British have evinced more optimism than the French regarding the prospects of greater European political and defense cooperation, the emphasis in Whitehall continues to be upon "cooperation between governments" and not upon any process of unification that would sweep away national borders or prerogatives.

The fact that Britain and France approach the institutions of the EEC from the shared premise of the primacy of national interests is clearly mirrored in the insistence of both governments that ultimate decision-making powers within the Community continue to reside in the Council of Ministers. Through the "Luxembourg" unanimity rule for voting, each national unit holds a potential veto over Community initiatives. Both London and Paris will use this veto power to protect their respective interests.

While agreeing on the abiding primacy of national interests in decision-making in the Community, however, there appear to be differences between the two countries in the degree to which each sees the Community serving its national interests, extant and potential. The French, throughout the history of the EEC, have not only combatted "supranational" tendencies in the Community, but more generally have tried to dampen any dynamic tendencies in that organization. Although M. Pompidou has taken a more tolerant stance toward the Community than his predecessor, he has shown no change in the fundamental French belief that a weak Community structure best serves to promote the French concept of European evolution.

Britain, in joining the EEC, appears to anticipate a rejuvenation of the Community institutions. Official thinking in Britain leans toward the view that a dynamic Community can be a valuable instrument for the promotion of both British and European interests. It remains to be seen whether this optimism reflects "neophyte enthusiasm" or British confidence in their ability to harness Community dynamics to British national interests.

Britain's apparent enthusiasm for its new European role also extends to defense cooperation in a European context, particularly in the Eurogroup, the coordinating body for European members of NATO. Recent achievements of this body have included the European Defense Improvement Program calling for a $1 billion expenditure by the European members of NATO through 1975 for force improvements, acceleration of work on the NATO infrastructure, and intra-alliance aid. In addition, the Eurogroup was instrumental in influencing the European NATO members to increase their defense budgets collectively by over $1 billion in 1972 as compared to 1971. Coupled to this was the "Europackage" of force improvements designed to improve NATO's conventional capabilities.

Britain has been a major motivating force behind the work of the Eurogroup. Its prominent role in this endeavor has reflected

Britain's emphasis upon NATO as the key framework of European defense efforts, as well as London's abiding belief in the reconcilability of intra-European and Atlantic cooperation. France is not a member of the Eurogroup, although the French have a standing invitation to enter into its deliberations "whenever they feel able to join us." (Carrington, 1972: 10). As will be noted below, former West German Defense Minister Helmut Schmidt, as Chairman of the Eurogroup in 1972, made special efforts to draw the French into the body. Yet, there is little hope that the invitation will be accepted. Paris continues to equate NATO with American dominance and, as such, cooperation within NATO and true European cooperation are viewed as mutually exclusive phenomena.

This brief review of basic British and French conceptions of the evolution of Europe and their respective approaches to the institutions of Western European unity suggests that a number of solid political obstacles still obtrude on the road toward possible Anglo-French nuclear cooperation. The obstacles relate in part to the similarity of views in Paris and London regarding the ultimate goals of European political evolution. Both governments stress the abiding sanctity of national prerogatives and essentially a "confederal" vision of Western European evolution. Yet Great Britain and France are pursuing different roads to this avowed objective.

The British favor a *linkage approach* to political unity. While insisting that ultimate decision-making power resides in the individual nation-states, London seeks to link economic, monetary, political, and defense cooperation into a coherent and interlocking whole. The British also insist that cooperation and unity can and must proceed at interlocking European and Atlantic levels.

France, on the other hand, pursues a *fragmentation approach* to cooperation. In line with President Pompidou's idea of a "division of labor" among the various European states, the French insist that the various spheres of European cooperation should remain geographically and functionally separated until the proper conditions for their linkage emerge. In particular, Paris remains unalterably opposed to meaningful defense cooperation in an Atlantic framework. Although the French recognize the importance of maintaining the American commitment to European security in the near-term future, the long-range policies of Paris are designed to move France and Europe toward a position that is less dependent on the United States.

These fundamentally divergent approaches, rather than differences over the narrower issues of European cooperation or unity, are likely to be major impediments to Anglo-French nuclear cooperation. The British insist on maintaining strong integrative links with the United States through NATO while strengthening political and defense collaboration in Europe. The French regard such linkage as anathema, both to French national interests and to their view of European evolution.

There has been speculation regarding institutional solutions for harmonizing the different approaches. An example of this is the notion that the Western European Union might serve as a mutually acceptable framework for Franco-British nuclear cooperation. The answer, however, does not seem to lie in institutional subterfuges but rather in fundamental national policies and attitudes. Unless some basic shifts in such policies and attitudes were to occur, the prospects for any political incentives and preconditions for a close Franco-British nuclear axis seem to be meager in the foreseeable future. There is, however, another major variable involved in the unity equation: namely, the Federal Republic of Germany (F.R.G.).

West German Attitudes and Policies

The "German problem" in NATO nuclear strategy has been a reflection of the broader "problem" within the alliance. Reduced to its essential nub, the problem has revolved around two questions: How can the Federal Republic of Germany be made a party to—and a part of—a viable alliance nuclear solution? What do the West Germans themselves want?

These questions in many respects dominated the "great nuclear debate" in NATO from the "Norstad Plan" of 1958 to the final failure of the MLF in 1966. Constantly hovering in the wings of that debate was the perceived peril that failure to satisfy West Germany's assumed demands for a share in NATO's nuclear strategy and decision-making might press that country to embrace an independent nuclear option of its own, with all of the frightening consequences that this might bring for the alliance and the future of Europe.

This "peril", however, has dwindled drastically. Moreover, the "German factor" is not as directly relevant to the problem of Franco-British nuclear cooperation as it was to the earlier search for a comprehensive NATO nuclear solution. Nevertheless, whatever scenario might be projected, the F.R.G., by dint of its political stature and economic power in Western Europe, is not likely to be a passive spectator to events. In the nuclear realm, moreover, Bonn's significance is enhanced by the fact that it has become in many ways the major spokesman for the non-nuclear members of NATO. The F.R.G.'s predilections will, therefore, bear importantly on the course of developments.

Background. From the time of the F.R.G.'s rearmament and its entry into NATO, West German attitudes on nuclear weapons generally, and strategic weapons in particular, have reflected a fundamental dilemma. Expressed in simplified terms, the two prongs of the dilemma have been the following: As the most exposed and vulnerable nation on NATO's Central Front, the F.R.G. has had a direct and vital stake in the creation and maintenance of an effective NATO nuclear deterrent against aggression from the east. At the same time, because of that very vulnerability, the F.R.G. has the most to fear from a failure of the deterrent, which might victimize it in one of several ways: (1) in the event of conflict in Europe, as the principal nuclear battlefield; and (2) in the event of a U.S.-U.S.S.R. conflagration triggered by events outside of Europe, as a major target of Soviet strikes against the forward bases of American nuclear power.

This dilemma sponsored a profound schizophrenia in West German thinking on nuclear matters that prevails to this day. The dilemma was exacerbated, beginning in the late 1950s, with the accelerating growth of a Soviet nuclear arsenal. It may be recalled that the NATO nuclear debate of 1958-1966 was prodded in good measure by a perceived West German penchant for a direct share in nuclear decision-making. In retrospect, this penchant was probably exaggerated in the eyes of fearful observers. During that period there was little in the way of a "nuclear consensus" in Bonn; rather opinion tended to be fairly sharply divided at the cabinet level, in the Bundestag, and within the major political parties themselves. If there were some general common denominators, at least within successive Adenauer and Erhard governments, they might be summarized as follows:

(1) In light of the dilemma noted, the West Germans desired some voice in NATO nuclear strategy—in the positive sense of insuring contingency use and influencing target lists, and in the negative sense of preventing a precipitate nuclear engagment that might devastate the two parts of Germany.

(2) Progressively, also, the West Germans desired political equality (euphemized in Bonn with the word *gleichberechtigung* or "equal privilegization") with Great Britain and France in the councils of the alliance. With growing West German economic strength and political self-confidence came resentments at the privileged roles that nuclear credentials seemed to confer upon Great Britain and (later and to a lesser extent) France, particularly in their dealings with the United States.

(3) From the West German vantage point, a central objective of any NATO nuclear arrangement was to tie American nuclear power more inextricably to the defense of Western Europe.

For all of these considerations, the Adenauer and Erhard governments tended to favor a "hardware solution" that would open to the F.R.G. a tangible share of any new NATO nuclear establishment. In any event, whatever positive ambitions the West Germans had injected into the nuclear debate, these were frustrated by the multilateral nuclear force (MLF) debacle in 1966. The MLF episode needs no recounting here. Suffice it to say that its meaning for the West Germans was not only a collapse of the NATO nuclear quest, but also one of profound political humiliation. Under 'American pressure, the Erhard government endorsed the MLF scheme despite doubts about its intrinsic merits and reluctance to risk a direct break with the Gaullist government in Paris—only to find itself "high and dry" when the

Johnson administration abruptly dropped the scheme in late 1964. The episode played no small part in the toppling of the Erhard government with its replacement by the Kiesinger-Brandt coalition in 1966.

Partly because of "MLF fatigue," but also for a number of circumstantial reasons, whatever "drive" there had been in Bonn for a nuclear solution subsided markedly after 1966. In the wake of MLF and the final evidence of France's go-it-alone policy came a general sense of resignation that the problem of "fifteen fingers on a trigger" was capable of solution. The newly created NATO Nuclear Planning Group (NPG) opened the door at least to West German participation in nuclear planning, if not decision-making. Finally, the West German government found itself increasingly confronting a priority issue—namely, the threat of American force withdrawals from Europe implicit in the balance-of-payments quarrels between Washington and Bonn.

Indeed, the only West German voices that could be heard on the nuclear issue in the late 1960s were those of the so-called German Gaullists like Franz Josef Strauss. Taking his cue in part from the alleged past American failures to satisfy European nuclear requirements. Strauss (1966, 1968) advanced a thesis which read roughly as follows: (1) Western Europe can no longer rely on the American nuclear guarantee for Europe; (2) the Soviet Union will be deterred from aggression and nuclear blackmail against Western Europe only by strategic nuclear capabilities in Western European hands; (3) in its own longer-run interest of remaining a vital nation, the F.R.G. cannot forfeit the general technological benefits that flow from nuclear technology; and (4) the only solution, therefore, resides in the creation of effective European strategic nuclear forces based upon Franco-British cooperation, hopefully assisted by the United States, and in which West Germany could play an important economic role. The fashioning of such a joint enterprise would also spur progress toward the political unification of Western Europe.

It bears noting that not only the West German "Gaullists" embraced this general view. Thus Professor Wilhelm Grewe (1967: 93), a foreign policy advisor to Chancellor Adenauer and succeeding governments, pronounced in 1967 a European political union with a common nuclear force as "the only option with a future."

Mainsprings of Attitudes of the Brandt Government. One of the first acts of the Brandt-Scheel coalition, after assuming power in October 1969, was the signing of the Nuclear Nonproliferation Treaty. Since that time, even the F.R.G.'s existing nuclear links with NATO have been deliberately downplayed in the declaratory policies of the Brandt government. This theme is unmistakable in successive White Papers issued by the West German Ministry of Defense. Indeed, it is fair to speak of a distinct "anti-nuclear bias" in the Brandt Administration—a bias that bespeaks a blend of ideological legacies, perceived policy imperatives and security conceptions.

The ideological legacies derive from the long and complex history of the ruling Social Democratic Party and particularly its postwar experience. There is no stark pacifist tradition within the SPD, but the party's ideological past has left residual antipathies to "power politics" in general and to "nuclear politics" in the modern setting. In the 1950s, having failed to prevent West German rearmament and integration into NATO, the SPD tried to launch a popular movement against the equipment of the Bundeswehr with nuclear delivery vehicles. The campaign "against the atomic death" failed, and soon thereafter the SPD executed a complete turn-about toward basic support of the government's NATO policies. Yet, the lingering antipathies toward "things nuclear" remain, particularly in the increasingly vocal left wing of the party.

Even weightier in the Brandt government's outlook are the perceived requirements of Ostpolitik. The government signed the NPT in deference to the insistent Soviet sine qua non that there could not be meaningful relations between the F.R.G. and the East until West Germany adjured once and for all any nuclear ambitions.[15] Even beyond that, however, the Brandt government has been sensitive to ostensible Soviet apprehensions of a German finger even close to the nuclear trigger and has seemingly gone out of its way to allay these apprehensions.

These policy considerations merge with an overall security

view of the Brandt administration that bears the primary imprint of former Defense Minister Helmut Schmidt. Suffice it to say that Schmidt, who is prominently identified with the right wing of the SPD, is less afflicted by ideological considerations than other members of his party or government. He not only has taken a realistic view of the role of nuclear weapons in deterrence, but has regarded them as essential to a "military balance" in Europe, which is the prerequisite both for West Germany's security and for a meaningful détente policy vis-à-vis the East. Yet, Schmidt has also been consistent in his view that within NATO only the United States can, and should, play this "balancing" role at the nuclear level. In the 1960's, Schmidt (1962: 82) argued vehemently against any direct West German access to nuclear weaponry, and he was an outspoken opponent of the MLF scheme in the Bundestag. He articulated his rationale in this respect as early as 1962:

> The Soviet Union cannot seriously feel itself threatened by the armament of the *Bundeswehr* so long as the *Bundeswehr* remains an integrated component of the overall defense of the West. . . . But the danger of the Soviet Union being provoked to preventive aggression will grow from the moment on when the Federal Republic appears able, if need be, to conduct an independent and autonomous foreign policy backed by the power of nuclear weapons.

Attitudes of the Brandt Government Toward Possible Anglo-French Nuclear Cooperation. At the official level in Bonn, there has been a conspicuous silence with respect to possible nuclear collaboration between France and Great Britain in the wake of the latter's entry into the EEC. Privately, members of the government and of its ruling parties invariably tend to disparage the likelihood of such collaboration and/or its potential fruits. Scornful reference is made to "mini-forces" that probably cannot reach their targets and in any event are likely to be left farther behind in the technological race. This disparagement is intended essentially for American ears. As such, it obscures some real and growing West German apprehensions, which relate to three major contexts.

Primary is the apprehension in Bonn that Franco-British

nuclear cooperation, if it should materialize, would hasten a decoupling of the American strategic deterrent from the defense of Europe and more generally a retrenchment of American military power from the continent.

This fear is addressed not only to Franco-British nuclear cooperation, but more generally to European military and technological cooperation *outside* NATO—i.e., in an EEC context. Defense Minister Schmidt, especially from his vantage point as Chairman of the NATO Eurogroup in 1972, has been a strong advocate of greater intra-European cooperation in the development and production of weaponry.[16] He has tried conspicuously to draw the French into such cooperation.[17] But the sharp criteria for such cooperation have been (1) that it take place within the NATO framework, and (2) that it be addressed to burden-sharing with the United States. Bonn has reiterated its opposition to any "militarization" of the expanded European Economic Community. Thus, when Prime Minister Heath made a statement in January 1972 pointing to improvements in European defense as the principal task of the future EEC, F.R.G. Foreign Minister Walter Scheel (1972) responded pointedly in a press conference:

> The Community must avoid invading the prerogatives of the Atlantic Alliance. In the foreseeable future nothing can replace NATO as the guarantee of the security of the Europeans. The Community has not grown together politically to a sufficient degree to aspire to a common defense policy.

West German apprehensions relate more broadly to a Franco-British "political axis" within Western Europe and the EEC. Without attempting to present a detailed analysis of the political intricacies of the London-Paris-Bonn triangle, some basic observations are in order.

While relations between the F.R.G. and France are today improved in comparison with their virtual severance in the mid-1960s, Paris and Bonn remain divided by abiding mutual suspicions, by monetary and economic issues, by rivalry in their détente policies, and by fundamentally opposed national security conceptions.

The Brandt government can claim major credit for paving the way for British entry into the EEC. Yet, it must be recalled that the British government that Bonn sought to admit into the Community was that of Harold Wilson's Labour Party. Without imputing sinister motives, it seems fair to suggest that the Brandt government foresaw in the entry of Great Britain, beyond the broadening of the Common Market, the arrival of a kindred government that could be counted upon to side with Bonn on the major issues in the Community.

The Conservative victory in Great Britain and the subsequent Paris-London rapprochement clearly have changed the political scenario from the vantage point of Bonn. Relations between Bonn and Paris, moreover, seem once again to be cooling in the light of Pompidou's apparent reversion to a greater degree of Gaullist "orthodoxy" and because of fundamental differences between France and the F.R.G. on negotiations with the East, particularly with respect to mutual balanced force reductions (MBFR). At the same time, the ties between London and Paris appear, gradually but perceptibly, to be warming up. There are comprehensible fears in Bonn that politically the F.R.G. may once again become the "odd man out" in Western Europe. These fears are mirrored in the apprehensive West German press coverage of symptoms of Franco-British rapprochement—e.g., the festive state visit by Queen Elizabeth to Paris in May 1972. Typical is the following speculation (*Frankfurter Allgemeine Zeitung*, 1972):

> On the one hand, Britain's entry [into the EEC] strengthens the Gaullist maxim that a unified Europe should not be a "melting pot" *à la* the United States. No one can imagine how the British Crown and a European government can be brought under one hat. At the same time, Britain's presence in Europe soothes French fears of the economic weight and political dynamic of the German partner.

There is uneasy recognition in Bonn that, notwithstanding the political obstacles in the way of a Franco-British nuclear entente, the unique nuclear credentials of the two countries in Western Europe do represent the potential underpinnings of a political "axis."

In the light of the above fears, the "worst of all possible worlds" in the view of the Brandt government would be active American cooperation with an Anglo-French nuclear combine—in other words, a tripartite American-British-French nuclear arrangement. To the extent that any British bid for nuclear partnership with France would require American blessings (or else mean a forfeit of existing British nuclear ties with the United States), any meaningful Anglo-French cooperation would entail some form of tripartite arrangement—direct or indirect, explicit or implicit—and the West Germans know it. An explicit American linkage with an Anglo-French nuclear enterprise would augur in West German eyes: (1) enhancement of "decoupling," if only because an American association along these lines would clearly signal a policy shift by Washington in favor of "Europeanization" of the NATO deterrent in Western Europe; and (2) in the political context, the establishment within NATO of the kind of *"directoire"* of nuclear powers aspired to by de Gaulle in the late 1950s that would consign the F.R.G. to a permanent junior status in the alliance.

West German fears in this context have focused primarily upon a Franco-American rapprochement. Indeed, behind the efforts of Defense Minister Schmidt to wean France toward greater cooperation in a NATO/Europe framework may well have been a preemptive intent. Members of the Brandt administration privately invoke the argument that American nuclear assistance to France would remove a major incentive for that country to "turn to Europe" for needed (presumably financial) help. They do not answer, however, the question whether such "European" (i.e., German) assistance would be forthcoming if applied for.

Prospects. The "German factor" weighs as heavily upon the possibility of a European nuclear force based upon Anglo-French cooperation, as it did upon NATO's search for an alliance-wide nuclear solution in the 1958-1966 period. The dimensions of the problem have changed, particularly with the F.R.G.'s accession to the NPT and its reduced penchant for an expanded role in nuclear weaponry and strategy. At the same time, however, the F.R.G.'s economic and political standing in the West European Community make it the most significant variable (outside the Washington-London-Paris "nuclear triangle") with respect to any European nuclear enterprise.

The present German government, particularly with its strengthened base as a result of the November 1972 elections, can be expected to view Anglo-French nuclear cooperation as antithetical to its basic security requirements and policy objectives in West and East. Should Anglo-French cooperation come about despite West German preventive efforts, the Brandt government in all probability would refrain from associating itself with a London-Paris nuclear axis.

There is another way in which the German issue might bear upon the prospects of Franco-British cooperation—namely, as a goad to such cooperation. This implies a scenario in which the F.R.G. grows so strong in political and economic muscle and independent policies that France and Great Britain conclude that they can block West German dominance in Western Europe only by combining their resources, including nuclear ones. This scenario, while conceivable, belongs at best to a remote future. In the more foreseeable time frame, especially as Great Britain "feels its way" into the EEC, London will, if anything, continue to heed West German predilections and sensitivities.

On balance, therefore, the German factor must be viewed as a weighty impediment to, rather than enhancement of, possible nuclear cooperation in a Franco-British, let alone broader European, framework.

Soviet Policy

The fact that the Soviet Union does not like independent nuclear capabilities in Western Europe requires little documentation. The Soviet campaign in this respect has been consistent. Yet, there have been interesting nuances.

Background. Moscow's campaign against European nuclear forces was not launched with any degree of intensity and concertedness until the latter part of the 1950s. Until 1955, the

Soviet preoccupation was to prevent the rearmament of the Federal Republic of Germany and its accession to NATO. By that time, Great Britain was fashioning nuclear weaponry. France, in that period, was in the initial development stages of its own weapons program.

After 1955, the drive to prevent the F.R.G.'s entry into NATO having failed, Moscow's propaganda guns were trained on the contingency of West German nuclear armament, either through nuclear sharing with the F.R.G.'s allies or by dint of an independent West German weapons development program. The Soviet campaign, in addition to injunctions against American "forward bases" and broadsides against Bonn, featured prominently the Rapacki and Gomulka plans for nuclear-free zones in Europe.

The campaign shifted into high gear in the early 1960s with the more generalized drive against "nuclear proliferation" against the background of the Sino-Soviet split, as well as the quickened search in NATO for a nuclear arrangement under broadened allied, including West German, auspices. The Soviet campaign sought to appeal primarily to the United States in light of "common superpower interests." In Europe, the ploys included (interestingly enough, in the light of current Soviet endeavors) the proposal to hold an all-European security conference, disparagement of French nuclear capabilities,[18] and an unremitting attack against Bonn's alleged nuclear ambitions.

The campaign continued after the collapse of the MLF scheme, albeit with noticeably reduced urgency. The key target was still the F.R.G.[19] By the time the NPT was opened for signature on July 1, 1968, in Washington, Moscow, and London, the idea of a NATO nuclear force was already well in limbo. On November 29, 1969, the Brandt government in Bonn signed the treaty.

Bonn's accession to the NPT in November 1969 removed the major sting from the European nuclear problem from Moscow's vantage point. Other developments in Western Europe in the late 1960s—notably the collapse of the MLF scheme and France's go-it-alone policies—further reduced the problem. The Soviet courtship of President de Gaulle demonstrated that the Soviet

Union could come easily to terms with a country that was a principal trailblazer of nuclear proliferation—and could do so notwithstanding the fact that the flatteries directed from Moscow toward Paris implicitly strengthened de Gaulle's argument that nuclear credentials mean prestige and influence in the modern international arena.

Soviet Views of Possible Franco-British Nuclear Cooperation. There has been relatively little direct reference to the possibility of Franco-British nuclear cooperation in Soviet official statements and the Soviet press. This does not necessarily reflect a lack of Soviet concern; indeed, the Soviet tactic, similar to that of the Brandt government, may well be to avoid undue attention to the problem in order to discourage its prospects.

There are other indications that Soviet concerns are real. These include indirect references to the problem. Thus, an article in November 1971, with the standard official imprimatur of "Commentator" (*International Affairs,* 1971: 65), hailed the failure of various schemes to create a joint NATO nuclear force and the F.R.G.'s accession to the NPT as "a political gain for the Warsaw Treaty countries," but warned that the task needed to be completed: "It is now important that all European countries should sign the Nonproliferation Treaty, and those which have already done so should back up their signatures with prompt ratification." The fact that "all European countries" refers essentially to France is made clear by glowing tributes elsewhere in the article (*International Affairs,* 1971: 64) to the growing accord and "mutual understanding between the Soviet Union and France, two European powers [that] has become part of the foundation of European peace."

Revealing in this context are Soviet plaudits to France as the guardian of national sovereignty principles. *Pravda* in May 1972 noted the appeals for greater political unification in the Western European arena, which it attributed to "attempts by international monopolies to rid themselves of the constricting national laws being adopted by the parliaments of some countries." It also referred to the subject of "European nuclear forces" and cited approvingly President Pompidou's "clear answer" to the effect that France would not be drawn, directly or indirectly, into the NATO framework. *Pravda* concluded: "Many political figures note that the weakening of national sovereignty can lead to ruinous political, economic and social consequences" (Kuznetsov, 1972).

The Soviet Union's concern over national nuclear forces in Western Europe was also mirrored in Soviet efforts in SALT. In SALT I, the Soviets drove hard for a U.S.-U.S.S.R. agreement to prohibit transfer by the superpowers of nuclear technology to other nations, but were successful in having such a nontransfer clause applied only to the treaty on ABM. More significant is the Soviet unilateral interpretation of the agreement of offensive weapons (an interpretation that was rejected by the United States) that seeks to void the agreement in the event of quantitative increases in current British and French strategic nuclear weapons. The Soviet intent clearly was to make these two countries, in effect, "silent signatories" to the agreement, or at least to force the United States to place a leash on the nuclear ambitions of its allies.

Prospects. Although the evidence is admittedly sporadic and circumstantial, it seems clear that, aside from preventing a German finger on the nuclear trigger, the Soviets assign reasonably high priority to the objectives of containing current British and French nuclear programs and preventing U.S. assistance to these programs; preventing nuclear collaboration between the two countries; and preventing a European nuclear force in a broader Western framework. It seems equally clear that the Soviet Union will continue to address to these objectives the political leverage at its command.

Moscow's methods will be indirect as well as direct. The indirect approach is likely to include the following broad and specific measures:

(1) Continued enhancement of a general climate of détente designed to reduce incentives in Western Europe for military collaboration in general, and for accelerated nuclear programs and cooperation in particular.

(2) Also in the interest of reducing such incentives, perhaps a more pronounced slowdown in the Soviet campaign to push the

American military presence from Europe—at least until such a time as Moscow feels that it has political inroads into Western Europe sufficient to influence and restrain developments there in its favor. If this is the Soviet calculus, it may even yield some limited interest in MBFR in order to prevent precipitate American drawdowns, which might galvanize the West European nations into concerted defense efforts.

(3) In SALT II, a renewed Soviet drive for a binding agreement with the United States on nontransfer of nuclear technology and for extending overall limitations on offensive weapons to British and French forces.

(4) Indirect political pressure against European nuclear cooperation through the F.R.G. and Scandinavian countries.

(5) Subtle tradeoffs. Thus, the Soviet Union may evince increasing willingness to enter into economic agreements with the EEC as a bloc in return for the "nonmilitarization" of that Community.

The Soviet arsenal of *direct* measures might feature the following:

(1) A continued divisive campaign in Western Europe—a campaign that is likely to focus particularly on France as a preferred Soviet negotiations partner in Western Europe and as the guardian of national sovereignty principles. This would be accompanied by a continuation of a low-keyed effort to induce France to sign the NPT.

(2) Repeated calls for nuclear disarmament or conclaves of the nuclear nations, with or without the participation of Peking.

(3) In the event of imminent decisions in London and Paris, full mobilization of communist and left-wing opinion in those countries against nuclear weaponry and collaboration.

(4) In the forums of CSCE (Conference on Security and Cooperation in Europe) or MBFR (mutual balanced force reductions), generalized proposals for comprehensive nuclear-free zones in Europe, as well as possibly direct bargaining gambits vis-à-vis the French and the British. There is already some speculation in Europe that the Soviets have stubbornly withheld the 600-plus MR/IRBMs emplaced in western Russia from the SALT negotiations partly in order to reserve these weapons as bargaining instruments vis-à-vis French and British forces.

Depending upon the evolution of the Franco-British relationship, Moscow is likely to resort to any or all of these measures to constrain British and French nuclear capabilities and to prevent their combining. For the foreseeable future, however, the Soviet Union is unlikely to invoke direct threatsmanship. The recent détente policies of the Soviet Union reflect in good part Moscow's recognition that its harsh reactions in past years often tended to galvanize the Western alliance rather than divide it. In the context of potential nuclear developments in Western Europe, moreover, the likely target list of Soviet military-political pressures has changed. In the past, Moscow could launch reasonable credible and effective pressure campaigns against the alleged nuclear ambitions of the F.R.G.—credible because the nuclear armament of West Germany was widely conceded in the West to be a "legitimate" security concern of the Soviet Union, and effective because the F.R.G., in light of its aspirations for reunification, was vulnerable to the Soviets militarily and politically.

France and Great Britain represent for the Soviet Union tactical and political problems of a different order. Neither country is as directly vulnerable to Soviet threatsmanship as the F.R.G. Both countries are nuclear powers, and Soviet attempts to brandish military threats against cooperation on their part would be received, and reacted to, as undisguised power plays. Moreover, the Soviets have wooed Paris by catering to de Gaulle's and his successors' mystique of France's strength through independent policies. Any effort by Moscow to wield direct military threats against Paris would tend to be not only counterproductive politically, but might also run the risk of reuniting France with NATO.

In short, the Soviet counter-campaign against any expansion or amalgamation of nuclear efforts in Western Europe would probably be waged energetically but with circumspection—at least until such a time as Moscow feels that it holds most of the military and political cards in Europe. Such a strategy probably will be continued, more broadly and with greater intensity, if Paris and London should arrive at a nuclear arrangement. In that event, the Soviet Union would probably accept the fait accompli of Franco-British cooperation grudgingly, at the same time shifting its priority to: (1) preventing or restraining American assistance to Franco-British nuclear projects, (2) exploiting the fact of Franco-British cooperation to widen the gulf between the nuclear and nonnuclear members of NATO, and (3) intensifying its efforts to sever the F.R.G. from its Western moorings in order to prevent any extension of the nuclear bridge to Bonn.

U.S. Policy and Legal Constraints

Aside from at-large political trends, the most important issue bearing upon Anglo-French nuclear cooperation is that of U.S. policy. Complicating this issue is the fact that "U.S. policy" in this context is not simply the function of the predilections of the Executive Branch of the U.S. government, but is constrained also sharply by statute and by congressional forces.

Constraints on British Nuclear Sharing. Legal restraints upon British nuclear sharing arrangements with France derive mainly from the 1958 U.S.-U.K. Agreement for Nuclear Cooperation. The restrictive provisions of this agreement, Articles V, VI, and VII, are based upon Section 123 of the U.S. Atomic Energy Act.[20]

The effect of these provisions is to prevent the United Kingdom from entering into sharing arrangements with other countries as long as it enjoys a special nuclear relationship with the United States and wants to sustain this relationship. As was discussed above, much of British nuclear and nuclear-oriented technology is either directly or indirectly derived from U.S. design and data. Indeed British dependence of the United States has been such that it would probably be extremely difficult to determine in British nuclear weapon systems where U.S.-derived design ends and that of British origin begins. Conceivably this commingling of data and materials would make violations of the 1958 agreement difficult to define; but the British are keenly aware that their nuclear relationship hinges not only on legalities, but also and more meaningfully on the disposition of the U.S. government—especially the Congress and the powerful Joint Committee on Atomic Energy.

The Joint Committee on Atomic Energy has played a crucial

role in the formulation of U.S. nuclear policy. Since its formation in 1946, the Committee has evinced sharp sensitivities to nuclear sharing. Instances where it has approved amendments to liberalize U.S. law and allow more sharing, such as in 1958, have been rare. Some of its most influential members began their tenure on the Committee in the late 1940s and 1950s, when fears regarding leakage of nuclear data were pervasive in Congress.[21] These old fears as well as the convictions of some of the Committee's staff members probably continue to sway the views of key members with respect to the question of liberalizing the conditions of the 1958 Agreement.

Indicative of these sentiments has been the irritation of leading Committee members over British ventures with West Germany and the Netherlands in developing centrifuge technology. In the early 1960s, the United States had turned over information about the process for producing nuclear fuel to the British. Later, the United States practically abandoned work in this particular area of fuel production while the British continued their own research and eventually sought a cooperative venture with the Federal Republic and the Netherlands. Reaction in the United States, and especially in the Joint Committee, was immediate and sharp. Even though U.S. experts concluded that the British had passed onto their European partners information that had been derived essentially from British research and development, some members of the Joint Committee were convinced that the British had passed on U.S. data and deceived the United States. Congressman Chet Holifield, Chairman of the Committee at the time of the incident, has been particularly adamant in trying to limit the sharing of technology on gaseous diffusion with U.S. allies (see, for example, Holifield, 1969: 56).

Thus, while there are legal avenues available for Anglo-French nuclear sharing, even within the context of the 1958 agreement, political hurdles imposed by Britain's relationship with the United States render such an endeavor remote. With the British nuclear program so closely tied to the U.S. program, and the present need of the United Kingdom to maintain the special relationship, there would seem to be, in the words of one expert (Pierre, 1972: 338), "a high value placed upon maintaining the spirit as well as the legal terms of the (1958) Agreement," with the British being careful not to act so as to arouse the Congress and the Joint Committee on Atomic Energy.

Impediments to U.S. Nuclear Cooperation with France. The United States holds today no "special relationship" of any kind with France. Indeed, to a large extent the restrictive interpretation of the MacMahon Act in the past and the attitudes of key members of the Joint Committee on Atomic Energy in the U.S. Congress were shaped by antipathy to French policies and nuclear ambitions.

A reversal of this policy in favor of U.S. assistance to French nuclear programs could be relevant to potential Franco-British cooperation in two ways: (1) by strengthening French nuclear programs and capabilities and thus contributing to more viable French *national* forces, and (2) by doing so without foreclosing the possibility of *eventual* nuclear cooperation between France and Great Britain or within a broader Western European framework. It is assumed here a priori that if the United States were to extend nuclear assistance to France, it would do so under the same (if not harsher) restrictions that have been applied to the British.

The main legal barrier to U.S.-French nuclear cooperation is the U.S. Atomic Energy Act. This act provides the legal basis for arrangements ranging from low-level assistance to the sharing of restricted data on nuclear weapons, as long as certain conditions are met. Only the transfer of nuclear warheads and bombs is prohibited. The act, however, requires that a recipient state has made "substantial progress" in its own nuclear weapons program and that it is making "substantial material contributions" to the common defense. These findings, notably the latter, are subject to political interpretation. Such agreements, furthermore, must not be, in the language of the act, an "unreasonable" risk to the United States. While the determination whether these conditions have been met rests with the President, the Atomic Energy Act requires that all such proposals be sent to the Congress and the Joint Committee on Atomic Energy for approval.[22] It is this procedural device that provides the opportunity for political prejudices and attitudes that spell the life or death of a proposed sharing agreement.

The Joint Committee on Atomic Energy, moreover, must be kept informed of all activities related to the development, utilization, and application of nuclear energy. The Committee, moreover, has the opportunity to make its influence felt also on such areas as the transfer of nuclear related technology.

One factor that will affect any high level technical agreement is the conviction in congressional circles that there is a horizontal as well as vertical dimension to proliferation. The first constitutes the actual transfer of nuclear weapons or nuclear weapons technology to a non-nuclear state. Vertical proliferation involves assisting a nuclear state with improving its capabilities. Such improvements, however, are regarded as destabilizing to the strategic environment about as much as horizontal proliferation would be. These ideas, which have become almost integral to the U.S. antiproliferation policy, find support in such places as the Foreign Relations Committee of the U.S. Senate and in the Joint Committee on Atomic Energy. The May 1972 SALT accords are bound to reinforce these deeply held views. There is, moreover, the concern felt in Congress and in other sectors of the government that American support to France's nuclear program could encourage proliferation.

A second obstacle against U.S. nuclear assistance to France's nuclear program derives from congressional concern with adhering to the 1963 Partial Test Ban Treaty. The treaty forbids atmospheric testing or activities that may contribute to such testing by another state. France has not yet signed the Partial Test Ban Treaty, nor is it likely to do so in the near future; it has, moreover, continued to conduct nuclear tests in the atmosphere. France's refusal to abide by the terms of the test ban treaty would merely provide Congress with another opportunity to oppose any proposed technical assistance agreements.

Finally, pervading much of the U.S. nuclear establishment is a strong mistrust of French security precautions. The French security system is frequently regarded as a porous one—and, indeed by some as a conveyor belt of information to the Soviet Union.

In short, the legal restrictions on potential U.S. nuclear cooperation with France—in the Atomic Energy Act and the Partial Test Ban Treaty—are flexible and may be surmounted. More telling obstacles, however, are inherent in deep-rooted political views in the United States, and particularly in the U.S. Congress, whose approval would be requisite to a change in U.S. policy.

Conclusions. It would be impossible as well as inappropriate in the scope of this study to undertake an analysis in depth, let alone a meaningful projection, of congressional and related attitudes in the United States relevant to potential U.S. nuclear relations with Great Britain and France. Yet, the evidence at hand supports at least some tentative and broad conclusions and projections:

(1) In the case of American tolerance of British nuclear cooperation with France, both the legal obstacles (posed by the U.S.-British Agreement of 1958) as well as the political barriers seem imposing and durable. Even should congressional attitudes toward British and French nuclear ambitions mellow and a less restrictive view of nuclear nonproliferation prevail, a major congressional concern will continue to be the abiding control over nuclear data released to Great Britain under the terms of the agreement.

(2) The British conceivably could sidestep the restrictive provisions of their agreement with the United States and relay to France nuclear information either covertly or with the justification that the given information is of British rather than of U.S. origin. Great Britain, however, is likely to undertake neither in face of the risk of severing the nuclear relationship with the United States.

(3) The obstacles to U.S. nuclear assistance to France are also formidable. Yet, the main obstacles remain political and procedural rather than legal. These barriers conceivably could be modified.

Possible Courses of Anglo-French Cooperation

It was suggested earlier that France should be able to muster an effective nuclear deterrent by the latter seventies or early eighties. Britain's nuclear credentials are clearly established; moreover, assuming that American assistance will continue to be forthcoming, Britain should be able to make the required improvements in its Polaris force within three or four years. A major boon for the continued viability of both strategic forces was the May 1972 SALT agreement and its limitations on the antimissile deployment in the United States and the Soviet Union. An expansion of Soviet missile defenses—no matter how questionable their effectiveness might be vis-à-vis the massive American nuclear striking power—would seriously compromise the credibility of the more modest British and French forces. At the very least, it would impose upon the programs of both countries staggering requirements of weapons sophistication —requirements that would tax the technological know-how as well as the economies of the two nations.

To this extent, the SALT accords, by holding forth to Paris and London a more tangible prospect that meaningful nuclear deterrent capabilities are within their reach, may act as a goal to the nuclear incentives in both countries. But the accords may well do so also in another important respect. A key, though frequently tacit, motive that originally pushed the nuclear programs in Great Britain and France was the desire for an insurance policy against the day when the American strategic umbrella might no longer protect Western Europe. The SALT accords, irrespective of their intrinsic merits and irrespective of the continued leeway they permit in the qualitative dimensions of the nuclear weapons race, clearly have placed the seal of parity of the U.S.-U.S.S.R. nuclear equation. And parity carries some inescapable implications for Western Europeans who contemplate the future evolution of their continent between two nuclear giants.

In short, it must be accepted as a foregone conclusion that the efforts in London and Paris to improve British and French nuclear capabilities will continue. Conceivably, the two allies might be able to reach their goals more quickly and economically if they were to combine or share resources for the development and production of nuclear weapons or coordinate the operations of their forces. Previous sections stressed the constraints on cooperation inherent in the differences in French and British strategic thought, the uneven levels in Anglo-French nuclear technologies, and the European political milieu. The effort will be made in this section to explore those modes of cooperation that might fit into those constraints.

Technological Cooperation

The nuclear technologies of Great Britain and France are to some extent complementary. The British have more experience than the French in the field of thermonuclear warheads and multiple reentry vehicles. Thanks to Anglo-American nuclear cooperation, Britain has a substantial lead over France in the development of nuclear propulsion reactors and other techniques associated with the Polaris submarine. On the other hand, indigenous rocketry development and production capability are more advanced in France. Then too, the French aerospace industry has made impressive strides. Conceivably, exchange of nuclear technology and joint nuclear development and production facilities would yield advantages to both. There are precedents for such cooperation, such as the Anglo-French collaboration in the development of the Concorde supersonic transport and some joint military systems as the Jaguar tactical aircraft and the Lynx, Gazelle, and Puma helicopters.

Yet some prominent difficulties stand in the way of this type of cooperation in the nuclear field. First of all, the British and French nuclear programs have reached different levels of maturity. Britain is primarily interested in improving the penetration capability of its submarine-launched missiles through hardening and penetration devices. The French have barely made a start in these technologies. What the French could offer the British—missile technology and limited testing facilities—the British obtained already from the United States at a much more sophisticated level. Where French testing facilities are concerned, as was discussed earlier, it is highly unlikely that Britain would be prepared to use those sites.

Moreover, it is difficult to equate the incentives for Anglo-French cooperation in systems such as the Concorde and Jaguar with possible incentives in the nuclear realm. The major lures for the former kind of cooperation were the promise of larger markets and through these, a way to reduce the final development and production costs. It is worth pointing out that the results have not rewarded those expectations; costs in these cooperative efforts have been very high and the markets sought have not materialized. In any event, the same kinds of economic incentives would not be compelling in the area of nuclear hardware.

The sensitive area of nuclear collaboration, moreover, raises another serious problem. If Britain were to give France access to some of its nuclear expertise, France would in effect be obtaining U.S.-derived technology. The French are not likely to take kindly to an arrangement that would put them into the position of recipient of second-hand U.S. technology through a British broker. Moreover, such an arrangement would tend to reemphasize the kind of special Anglo-American relationship which has been anathema in Paris. If France decided to opt for U.S. technology, there is no reason why it would not prefer to turn to Washington directly rather than deal through Great Britain.

From a British vantage point, other inhibitions bear upon the question of giving France access to British nuclear data. These inhibitions relate precisely to the special relationship with the United States—a subject that was explored in the previous chapter. Without explicit American encouragement and approval, Britain would be unlikely to engage in technological cooperation with a third party and risk cutting its nuclear link with the United States.

Operational Coordination

If the prospects for meaningful Anglo-French technological cooperation in the nuclear field appear dim, the two countries might nevertheless find other ways to enhance their overall nuclear capabilities. In order to maximize the effectiveness of their strategic forces or reducing the vulnerability of their seaborne nuclear elements, the French and British could engage in operational coordination of their forces. Such joint efforts could conceivably include:

(1) Coordination of deployment periods and overhaul schedules of nuclear-armed submarines. Both countries have equipped their submarines with nuclear reactors which require major overhaul or replacement after three years of operation. Minor refitting is required after each eight to ten weeks of patrol. If the British and French were to coordinate their shipyard overhaul cycles to prevent or limit overlapping periods, they could maximize the number of submarines on station at any given time.

(2) Coordination of antisubmarine warfare (ASW) operations to expand the areas of control and avoid possibilities of mistaken identity. As a start, the two countries might coordinate their ASW activities in the English Channel. The British are already in charge of ASW operations in the Channel under the NATO structure. From a French vantage point, the Channel is a vital route of transit between their home port at Brest and their deployed positions in northern waters. In view of this, the Channel lends itself as a logical first choice for the coordination of ASW activities.

(3) British assistance to France with a training and recruitment program for nuclear powered submarine crews. France has still a number of problems in training personnel with the highly technical skills and psychological stamina required for manning nuclear powered submarines. The British with their larger operational base and experience could be of valuable assistance to the French. This mode of cooperation is primarily a one-way street, which Britain

might wish to take for more indirect political gains, but only if an explicit American blessing were forthcoming.

(4) Cooperation in strategic planning. The institution of some type of an Anglo-French strategic study group to exchange and explore strategic concepts and to select areas of mutual concern for further study would help to build an atmosphere of mutual confidence. Continuing contacts between French and British staffs would facilitate an orderly approach to identifying those areas that are susceptible to cooperation and exclude those that are not. Regular exchanges in such a forum would pave the way for coordinated planning for the individual use of the two national forces.

(5) Exchange of intelligence data on targets in the Soviet Union and on Soviet defense systems. Information on the characteristics of Soviet ABM systems and ASW techniques would enhance the chances of penetration and the survivability of the Anglo-French strategic forces. In light of Britain's highly professionalized intelligence operations and access to U.S. intelligence and targeting information, this type of exchange would be particularly beneficial to the French. Precisely because of Britain's ties with U.S. intelligence operations, this type of Anglo-French cooperation would be unrealistic to contemplate without clear American approval.

(6) Coordination of the deployment of nuclear submarines. At first sight, this appears to be a logical option to expand the coverage of the Soviet Union by the French and British forces. But in order to achieve effective results, such coordination would have to be based on joint targeting and shared doctrine for the use of the forces. Whether the acceptance of truly joint targeting and doctrine is a possibility remains to be seen.

(7) Coordination of targeting. By eliminating possible duplication in target coverage, a joint targeting plan would increase the effectiveness of British and French forces. Without abandoning their own national targeting plans based on a countervalue strategy, the British have also accepted a targeting array designed in conjunction with SACEUR's strike plan. Superficially, there is no reason why the French could not retain their own target scheme and accept in addition joint targeting with their British counterparts to maximize the destructive potential of the two forces. Such cooperation would neither violate French beliefs that a multiplicity of nuclear decision-making centers gravely complicates the problems for the Soviet planner, nor compromise France's ultimate hold over its own nuclear arsenal. The British may more readily accept the concept of joint targeting than the French, who, conditioned by past experiences of U.S. efforts to drive France out of the nuclear club, would be suspicious that such a joint plan constituted a cover

for efforts to control French nuclear forces. France would require, therefore, tangible evidence of good faith, such as perhaps some sharing in American—or British—nuclear technology, or even access to U.S. underground testing sites. Whether it could be politically feasible for the United States to make such an offer, would depend on (a) whether the U.S. administration could persuade the Congress that the benefits of an enhanced deterrent capability in Europe are worth the political price of providing access to U.S. technology or extending of U.S. testing facilities to France, and (b) a number of factors related to U.S.-U.S.S.R. interactions that will be explored in the next chapter.

Prospects

The serious obstacles that will prevent technological cooperation between Britain and France also pertain to higher levels of operational collaboration. Yet even the more modest forms of concerted operational activity that do not require a dilution of national control will need to await appropriate timing. President Pompidou is already under attack from the extreme left and right for abandoning Gaullist principles of retaining full national independence and for moving surreptitiously toward the NATO fold again (see, for example, *Le Monde*, 1972b). The British are also likely to be prudent. Certainly they will wish to avoid ruffling congressional feathers in the United States if they hope to retain whatever U.S. support they enjoy for their nuclear program.

Thus, the prospects for meaningful cooperation in the immediate future are remote. Such prospects as there are depend upon how rapidly the French will be able to reach approximately the level of the British in nuclear force development. Superimposed on this constraint are Anglo-French perceptions of developments external to Britain and France—e.g., superpower interactions in SALT and the domestic climate in the United States as it affects the status of American forces in Europe. In the final analysis, the key variable in the prospects for Anglo-French nuclear collaboration is American policy.

One clear implication for the Europeans is that, to the extent that in the past American strategic superiority served to redress

Soviet military advantage on the ground in Europe, parity has the effect of sealing imbalance at the theater level, with all the military and political portents that this may hold. In particular, Soviet parity at the intercontinental level renders more conspicuous the shadow cast by massive Soviet conventional forces and the 600-plus intermediate and medium-range missiles in western Russia aimed at Western Europe.

Thus, no matter how fervently British official spokesmen may join their continental colleagues in arguing that nothing has really changed in the European security equation and that the American strategic commitment stands as credibly as ever, and no matter how much hope may be vested in détente, uneasiness is growing in London, Paris, and elsewhere. For this reason, the arguments in favor of "insurance capabilities" in European hands are bound to intensify, even if such arguments are rarely expressed openly for fear of hastening an American withdrawal from Europe or of disturbing the climate of détente.

Anglo-French Nuclear Cooperation and United States Interests

The basic phenomenon of a European nuclear force is not a new apparition on U.S. foreign policy horizons. It has lingered in the background of a fundamental dilemma that has long dogged American policies in NATO and that pervaded the great nuclear debate of the sixties in the Western alliance. In terse form, the dilemma might be described as follows:

On the one hand, the United States has been sensitive to the nuclear ambitions of its NATO allies and to the political mainsprings of these aspirations. In good part motivated by this understanding, the Eisenhower administration in the late 1950s undertook to assist its British ally in the development of a national nuclear capability. The United States has also recognized, albeit with varying degrees of approbation and skepticism, the strategic concerns that have kindled these ambitions—notably the desire by West European nations for direct control of deterrent capabilities that might insure survival in the ultimate contingency.

On the other hand, the specter of nuclear proliferation has long haunted U.S. officialdom. Although this specter has been viewed from Washington in a global perspective and as a global danger, it has most sharply influenced U.S. attitudes and policies toward national nuclear ambitions in Western Europe.

This dilemma and a myriad of related military and political issues have been responsible for some pronounced veers in past American policy toward Western Europe. At the risk of oversimplification, one might describe the first ten years of NATO as a period of *laissez-faire* in American nuclear policies toward the European NATO allies. This was the decade in which nuclear weapons were being deployed by the United States to Western Europe in burgeoning quantity and variety; when the United States embraced the strategy of massive nuclear retaliation, when the decision was made to share U.S. nuclear expertise with Britain; and when nuclear delivery vehicles were made available to U.S. allies. The latter part of this period, beginning with General Lauris Norstad's concept of a NATO-Europe as a fourth atomic power, also witnessed the start of a sincere U.S. effort to satisfy European nuclear aspirations.

The year 1961 witnessed a sharp shift in U.S. policy. The effort to meet European nuclear ambitions and to fashion an equitable nuclear solution for the alliance continued. Yet, clearly the weight of priorities in Washington in the early 1960s veered away from the objective of meeting European nuclear aspirations and toward the goal of halting nuclear proliferation. The denouement came in the U.S.-proposed multilateral nuclear force (MLF) and the initiatives attending this ill-fated scheme. Without imputing sinister motives, it seems fair to say that behind the MLF and other schemes advanced by the United States in NATO during that period lay not so much the aim of giving the West European allies a real share in the control of nuclear hardware, but rather the opposite—namely, the objectives of (1) gaining closer NATO and thereby American control of the independent British nuclear force, (2) discouraging the French nuclear program, and (3) preempting the feared contingency of a national nuclear enterprise in West Germany. Faced with strong resistance in Europe, the Johnson administration dropped the MLF proposal, particularly when it appeared that some form of consultation within the alliance on nuclear strategy and planning would help to meet German concerns. The result was the NATO Nuclear Planning Group.

The American drive for nonproliferation found its reward in the Nuclear Nonproliferation Treaty, which has been endorsed by a majority of nations (albeit not by France, China, and several key "nuclear nth countries"). The question now arises: to what extent, if any, have American interests changed in the interim?

U.S. Policy Interests During the 1960s

Without presuming to define U.S. interests categorically, it may be suggested that the problem and attendant U.S. interests have indeed undergone change. The salient changes are the following:

American policy in the 1960s sought to prevent of halt the emergence of independent nuclear capabilities in Europe. There are now two independent nuclear forces in Western Europe: one of these, the French force, is independent not only of American control, but even of palpable American influence. To this extent, U.S. objectives of the sixties foundered.

Moreover, the problem presented by possible Anglo-French cooperation is no longer one of nuclear proliferation, if "proliferation" is defined as the accession to military-nuclear power by a country not now so endowed. It might even be argued that Anglo-French cooperation, if it were to be carried to the ultimate step of a single centralized command and control system, would promote the goals of nonproliferation by *reducing* the existing number of nuclear forces under independent national control.

A more important question, however, involves the fundamental American interests vis-à-vis its European allies, its relations with the Soviet Union, and more broadly, its role in the global environment. Have these fundamental interests changed?

The basic dilemma that confronted the United States in the early sixties consisted, on the one hand, of the aspirations of its allies for a share in the nuclear decision-making of the alliance, and, on the other hand, of the dangers of nuclear proliferation —and in particular of West German accession to nuclear weaponry. Faced with this dilemma, the United States cast a priority choice for nonproliferation. Notwithstanding the traumas that this choice introduced into alliance relations, it was comprehensible in the context of the times and perceived American national interests. The United States in the 1960-1965 period became progressively and disconcertedly aware of a new fact of life that in its magnitude seemed to blanket all other national interests—namely, the reality of Soviet nuclear-tipped missiles aimed at American targets. In deference to that reality, the conviction solidified in Washington that, while the American nuclear deterrent against Soviet aggression had to be maintained, only an American President should in the final analysis be the one to cast the fateful decisions that might expose his country to a nuclear strike. In the alliance arena, this conviction meant that American control over the instruments of nuclear conflict should remain as undiluted as possible.

The American choice was influenced also—although to a lesser degree—by perceptions in Washington of allied nuclear ambitions. The European quest for nuclear hardware under European possession and control had intensified in the period of the "missile gap" (roughly 1958-1961), when the American strategic deterrent seemed thoroughly discredited by an assumed Soviet primacy in space and missile power. Yet, the ensuing years and their intelligence yield disproved such beliefs. The American strategic nuclear panoply, although compromised by Soviet advances, continued supreme into the latter part of the sixties. From the American vantage point, the European appetite for a share in nuclear decision-making could not, or should not, be as acute as before.

On the basis of these imperatives and assumptions, the United States in the sixties evolved a "package approach" toward NATO that consisted essentially of the following policy thrusts:

(1) Raise the "nuclear threshold" of potential conflict in Europe through a strategy that emphasized conventional defenses;

(2) Reiterate the American strategic commitment to the defense of Western Europe through the continued deployment of American nuclear power, although a power more tightly controlled; and

(3) Satisfy European nuclear ambitions through essentially token arrangements of shared hardware and planning.

The degrees of success and failure of this American approach of the sixties will only be judged in the longer light of history. The approach reaped ostensible success when NATO formally accepted the strategy of flexible response in 1967. In the realm of "nuclear diplomacy", the scoreboard is more confused. A distinct casualty of the American policy was the defection of France from the integrated commands of the alliance and its go-it-alone nuclear policy (although it conceivably might be rationalized that President de Gaulle would have taken this path in any event). On the ostensible success side was the accommodation by the remainder of the alliance to American nuclear predominance—an accommodation that seemed to be reflected in the European acceptance of the NATO Nuclear Planning Group and in the apparent satisfaction of demands for a more tangible European role in NATO nuclear strategy.

In any event, the "great debate" in the alliance over nuclear hardware and strategy waned conspicuously after 1966. Whether this was the result of renewed European confidence in American protection, as Americans liked to believe, or of "MLF fatigue," as some Europeans will contend, is a question primarily of interest to historians. What is more important for the future of the U.S.–European relationship is that the scenario has changed dramatically in the intervening years.

The most salient change has been twofold: the deep thrust by the Soviet Union toward a position of strategic-nuclear parity with the United States and the shifting American domestic temper. In explicit deference to both of these phenomena, the United States has recast its global policy. However variously it may be interpreted, the Nixon Doctrine prescribes a more selective and gingerly approach by the United States towards its global interests.

NATO and the Nixon Doctrine

The Nixon Doctrine calls for a new "partnership" relationship between the United States and Western Europe. The form that this "partnership" is to take has yet to be spelled out clearly in Washington, but a recurrent theme in President Nixon's policy statements refers to a politically more cohesive Western Europe able to shoulder a large share of its own defense responsibilities. The presumed objective, in short, is a greater measure of Western European self-reliance. At the same time, however, the Nixon administration has resolutely beaten back congressional initiatives aimed at easing the U.S. burden in NATO—namely, the 300,000-odd American forces stationed in Western Europe.

If there is thus an apparent disparity between American policy blueprint and policy action, this can be explained in terms of sensitivity by the U.S. administration to the problem of how to manage profound change in transatlantic relations without, in the process, opening irreparable cracks in the very foundations of the alliance. There is a recognition in Washington that, precisely to the extent that the credibility of the American strategic commitment to the defense of Western Europe is withering in the shadow of U.S.-U.S.S.R. parity, the American force presence in Western Europe is embraced all the more doggedly by Europeans as the major remaining token of America's nuclear guarantee. The conclusion follows that American force reductions at this juncture, particularly when unaccompanied by commensurate Warsaw Pact reductions and in the absence of a NATO-wide agreement on an alternative strategy and force posture for the alliance, could trigger an explosive crisis of confidence in NATO.

The decision by the Nixon administration to hold firm against pressures for force withdrawals from Europe thus has bought precious time for the alliance. The impending negotiations for mutual and balanced force reductions in Europe (MBFR) may buy additional time. Yet, the available time is by no means unlimited. Even if Senator Mansfield and other proponents of U.S. force reductions in Europe can be held at bay, the American force presence will be increasingly at the mercy of a dwindling defense budget and soaring military manpower costs in the United States.

The time that has been purchased must be exploited to define and to implement the U.S.-European partnership concept. Other considerations lend urgency to this task. The United States and its allies face a demanding and complex round of East-West negotiations in SALT II, the Conference on Security and Cooperation in Europe (CSCE) and MBFR. There can be little doubt that the Soviets will use these negotiations to strike against the transatlantic links in NATO. This prospect looms particularly in SALT, where the Soviets already have made amply clear their intention of making American forward-based weapons systems (FBS) in NATO prime negotiations targets. So long as NATO remains handcuffed to its present posture—and particularly to the legend of an unstinted and permanent American strategic nuclear guarantee of Western Europe—the alliance lies critially and perhaps fatally vulnerable to Soviet divisive thrusts. At the same time, the alliance is deprived of the kinds of bargaining assets and leeway that might achieve meaningful and equitable agreements with the Soviet Union and the Warsaw Pact.

There are a number of alternative solutions to the problem of an increasingly tenuous NATO posture. A common denominator of these alternatives is the evolution in Western Europe of a reasonably effective nuclear deterrent under European control. Such a European force would have to be based on the French and British nuclear forces. Eventually these forces would have to be coordinated in a wider European framework, preferably in NATO, but otherwise in some type of revived Western European Union structure, in order to demonstrate allied cohesion and resolve vis-à-vis the Soviet-dominated Warsaw Pact. There is no reason to insist that either France or Britain would have to surrender ultimate national control over their forces or jettison their own national targeting plans. The American strategic deterrent, before the dawn of nuclear parity, has ably protected Western Europe, yet always remained under U.S. control.

The existence of meaningful nuclear capabilities in European hands would help to offset the loss of West European confidence, if a perception of decoupling were to prevail in European capitals. It could go far toward neutralizing the effects of that perception and could render the process less dangerous and less painful. It would strengthen West European resilience against Soviet coercion, particularly if truly effective nuclear forces would be fashioned gradually and with American support. Such an evolution in the Western defense posture would then permit a more rational approach to the question of American forces stationed in Europe—forces that have always been valued by the European allies as much for their tangible evidence of the U.S. nuclear commitment as for their direct military value. This evolution, rather than a precipitous unilateral—or multilateral—withdrawal, would preserve Western Europe as the necessary frontier of American freedom.

The development of more credible European nuclear deterrent

forces *alone* would by no means provide the complete answer to the faltering Western defense posture; nor would such a development *by itself* permit withdrawals of American troops. Suffice it to say here that qualitative improvements in the present conventional and tactical nuclear forces in Europe and in their deployment would also be required to insure the political credibility and military effectiveness of the total deterrent and defense posture of Western Europe. But the existence of meaningful nuclear capabilities in European hands would give the United States and the alliance more generally some hedge against the decline of the credibility of the American nuclear guarantee.

Moreover, the development of Anglo-French nuclear forces would not necessarily be incompatible with American objectives in SALT. Both superpowers have a vital interest in strategic stability, as their efforts in SALT reflect. The rise of fully independent European nuclear power centers, devoid of any U.S. influence, could jeopardize such efforts. Much more in harmony with the SALT goals would be the emergence of European nuclear forces that, by dint of U.S. support, would be amenable to U.S. influence.

Thus, a case can be made for the proposition that the advantages of credible European nuclear capabilities to evolving American interests outweigh the risks that ten years ago preoccupied American policy. Indeed the emergence of such indigenous capabilities in Western Europe appears to be in accord with the logic of the Nixon Doctrine.

While the emergence of credible nuclear capabilities in Western Europe could support U.S. interests in West European security, the outlook for Anglo-French nuclear collaboration is far from bright. The difference in strategic concepts in London and Paris, the asymmetry in nuclear technology, the absence of any compelling economic incentives, and the political constraints pressing against cooperation have been explored earlier. This road to enhancing the Western deterrent posture in Europe does not appear to be a promising one for the near future. A more palpable alternative in the short run may lie in American bilateral support to Britain and France. The United States already provides a measure of support to Britain's nuclear program and may wish to expand its assistance. Washington may also wish to consider establishing gradually a nuclear relationship with Paris. True, the domestic obstacles to such a course in the United States are considerable, and it entails risks for intra-Alliance and East-West relations. Yet, these risks do not inhere in the policy option itself; rather they are a function of how the policy would be implemented. In any event, the potential risks seem overshadowed by the much greater dangers portended by divergent trends that now assert themselves in the Western Alliance.

NOTES

1. General Charles Ailleret (1967) argued that France's defense policy had to be designed against a threat coming from all directions, instead of emanating from only the East. Ailleret's arguments, which had been presented primarily for political reasons, were implicitly or explicitly rejected by several strategists and analysts, including General Michel Fourquet (1969); Edmond Combaux (1968); Guirec Doniol (1971).

2. Even Michel Debré, one of the staunchest Gaullists, has repeatedly stressed the necessity for American troops to remain in Europe. See, for example, Debré (1972b).

3. Britain committed additional air reinforcements to the continent and increased its naval cooperation in the Mediterranean. See Great Britain (1969).

4. See, for example, the report on Michel Debré's speech (1972a) to reserve officers in March 1972. See also the report in Le Monde (1972a) on French perceptions of the threat.

5. Even Michel Debré, one of the staunchest Gaullists, has repeatedly stressed the necessity for American troops to remain in Germany; see Debré (1972b).

6. British nuclear thinking and efforts during the war years are reviewed in Pierre (1972).

7. For early French views of the military utility of nuclear weapons, see Ailleret (1954); Chassin (1954); and Debau (1955).

8. See, for example, the justification of the nuclear program presented by the French government and its supporters in the debates on the military appropriations in the National Assembly in October 1960 (France, 1960). These points were faithfully repeated in debates in following years.

9. According to Denis Healey (1970: 1), the period of conventional resistance is more likely to be under five than under ten days. Others (e.g., Brown, 1972: 126) have suggested four to six days.

10. There is, however, a small minority of prominent military leaders who think it essential to prepare for a sustained conventional resistance —partly because they fear collateral damage, partly because they fear escalation once the nuclear firebreak is passed. See, for example, General Sir John Hacket, former Commander of Northern Army Group (1970), and Lord Mountbatten, former Chief of Defense Staff (1970). Advocates of this view find allies among those who seek to redress the balance of the services in favor of the army.

11. Since 1962, France has organized its forces into three operational systems of forces: (1) the strategic nuclear forces; (2) the forces of maneuver with the mission to contain an enemy that might attack France or its allies in or outside Europe; and (3) the forces for operational defense of the territory (DOT) with the mission of direct defense of France. French forces in Germany are part of the forces of maneuver.

12. The debate was summarized by Planchais (1965) and by Giniger (1965).

13. The details of French politics with respect to the development of the French nuclear capability can be found in Scheinman (1965) and in the analyses of two of the leading actors in the French atomic program, General Charles Ailleret (1968) and Bertrand Goldschmidt (1962).

14. By comparison, the U.S. projection for expenditures for nuclear forces in FY 1973 is 10.6! of the total U.S. defense budget. Figure extracted from Laird (1972: 189, Table 1).

15. Thus, Foreign Minister Scheel (1969) explained (somewhat euphemistically) in the Bundestag that failure to sign the NPT "would limit the freedom of our German (G.D.R.) and Eastern policy."

16. Thus, the session of the Eurogroup in Brussels on May 23, 1972 was preoccupied almost exclusively with these subjects. See the "Final Communiqué" of the meeting in the press release (*Mitteilung an die Presse*) of the Defense Ministry in Bonn dated May 24, 1972.

17. According to press reports (*Frankfurter Rundschau*, 1972), Schmidt has been trying privately to persuade French Defense Minister Debré that future French weapons exports–e.g., of Mirages and AMX-30 tanks– might suffer under a pooled competition of the other European NATO countries in weapons development.

18. Thus, a *Pravda* commentary (Nekrasov, 1963) described the *force de frappe* as too modest ever to be "in a position to change the balance of the world."

19. At a news conference in London on February 9, 1967, Premier Kosygin (quoted in *Pravda,* February 11, 1967) bluntly emphasized that

as for the Federal Republic, I must say that it will have to join the agreement on nonproliferation whether it wants to or not. We will not allow the Federal Republic of Germany to have nuclear weapons and we will take all measures to prevent it from obtaining the possibility of possessing these weapons. We say this with full determination.

20. Article V, which sets down the conditions of nuclear sharing, requires that information communicated or materials given to a recipient shall be used exclusively by it, and only for the preparation and implementation of defense plans in the mutual interests of both countries. Article VI states that classified information communicated or materials transferred under the agreement cannot be given by the recipient state to any unauthorized persons beyond its jurisdiction. Article VII, moreover, prohibits the communication of information or transfer of material to any nation or international organization *unless* authorization is given by the source party. The Joint Committee on Atomic Energy has maintained that, before the U.S. government may give such permission, congressional approval is necessary. The Committee has felt that such a decision would substantially modify the original agreement and thus require the additional approval.

21. Dates of appointment or association with the Committee: John O. Pastore, Chairman, 1972; Melvin Price, Vice Chairman, 1946; Chet Holifield, 1946; Henry Jackson, 1955; and Craig Hosmer, 1958.

22. The proposed agreement for cooperation, together with the President's approval and determination that the proposed agreement will not create an unreasonable risk to the United States, must be sent to the Congress. No proposal will become effective if Congress vetoes it by a concurrent resolution; otherwise, after a period of at least 30, but not more than 60 days, the agreement takes effect.

82

REFERENCES

AILLERET, C. (1968) L'Aventure Atomique Française. Paris: Editions Bernard Grasset.

——— (1967) "Défense 'dirigée' ou défense 'tous azimuts.'" Revue de Défense Nationale (December): 1923-1932.

——— (1964) "Opinion sur la théorie stratégique de la 'flexible response.' " Revue de Défense Nationale (August): 1323-1340.

——— (1957) "Illusion on réalité de l'arme absolue." Revue de Défense Nationale (October): 314-325.

——— (1954) "L'arme atomique arme à bon marché." Revue de Défense Nationale (October): 314-325.

BLACKMAN, R.V.B. (1972) Jane's Fighting Ships 1972-1973. London.

BROWN, N. (1972) European Security 1972-1980. London: Royal United Services Institute.

CARRINGTON (1972) "The Eurogroup." NATO Review (January-February).

CHASSIN, L. M. (1954) "Réflexions stratégiques sur la guerre d'Indochine." Revue de Défense Nationale (December).

CLIFFE, T. (1972) Military Technology and the European Balance. London: International Institute for Strategic Studies.

COMBAUX, E. (1968) "Défense tous azimuts. Oui, mais . . . " Revue de Défense Nationale (November): 1600-1618.

DEBAU, E. J. (1955) "Les armes atomiques et la défense nationale." Revue de Défense Nationale (July): 5.

DEBRE, M. (1972a) Speech quoted in Le Monde (March 8).

——— (1972b) Statement quoted in Le Monde (February 17).

——— (1972c) "La France et sa défense." Revue de Défense Nationale (January).

——— (1971) "France's global strategy." Foreign Affairs (April).

DONIOL, G. (1971) "Demain: armée de mer ou marine nationale." Revue de Défense National (April): 558-565.

ELY, P. (1957) "Notre politique militaire." Revue de Défense Nationale (April).

FONTAINE, A. (1972) Article in Le Monde (February 11).

FOURQUET, M. (1969) "Emploie des différents systèmes de forces dans le cadre de la stratégie de dissuasion." Revue de Défense Nationale (May): 757-767.

France (1972) Livre Blanc sur la Défense Nationale. Paris.

——— (1960) Journal Officiel, Assemblée Nationale, Debats Parlémentaires (October 13, 18, 19).

Frankfurter Allgemeine Zeitung (1972) "Der Anfang eines neuen Europa." (May 16).

Frankfurter Rundschau (1972) "Die Euro-Gruppe und die Franzosen." (May 4).

GALLOIS, P. (1961) The Balance of Terror. Boston: Houghton-Mifflin.

GERARDOT, P. (1957) "L'impasse nécessaire." Revue de Défense Nationale (April).

German Defense Ministry (1972) Press Release (Mitteilung an die Presse) (May 24).

GINIGER, H. (1965) Article in The New York Times. (January 19).

GOLDSCHMIDT, B. (1962) L'Aventure Atomique. Paris: Arthème Fayard.

Great Britain (1969) Statement on the Defence Estimates (Cmnd. 3927).

––– (1957) Defence: Outline of Future Policy: 1957 (Cmnd 124).

GREWE, W. C. (1967) "Ueber den Einfluss der Kernwaffen auf die politik." Europa-Archiv (February 10).

GRIFFITHS, E. and M. NIBLOCK (1970) Towards Nuclear Entente.

HACKET, J. (1970) Letter to The Times. (February 19).

HEALEY, D. (1970) "Does the strategy of flexible response need modifying? " London: Royal United Services Institute Seminar Report.

HEATH, E. (1970) Old World, New Horizons: Britain, the Common Market, and the Atlantic Alliance. London: Oxford Univ. Press.

––– (1969) "Realism in British Foreign Policy." Foreign Affairs 48 (October).

HOLIFIELD, C. (1969) Statement in U.S. Congress, Joint Committee on Atomic Energy. Future Ownership of the A.E.C.'s Gaseous Diffusion Plants. Hearings (July 8, 9; August 5, 7, 8): 56.

International Affairs (Moscow) (1971) "For a military détente in Europe." (November 1).

International Institute for Strategic Studies (1972) The Military Balance 1972-1973. London: International Institute for Strategic Studies.

KELLY, G. A. (1960) "The political background of the French A-bomb." Orbis (Fall): 284-306.

KOHL, W. (1971) French Nuclear Diplomacy. Princeton: Princeton Univ. Press.

KOLODZIEJ, E. (1972) "France ensnared: French strategic policy and bloc politics after 1968." Orbis 4 (Winter).

KOSYGIN, A. (1967) Statement at a news conference February 9, quoted in Pravda (February 11).

KUZNETSOV, N. (1972) "Behind the facade of supranationalism." Pravda (May 30).

LAIRD, M.L. (1972) Statement of Secretary of Defense Melvin R. Laird Before the Senate Armed Services Committee on Fiscal Year 1973 Defense Budget and Fiscal Years 1973-1977 Program (February 15). Washington, D.C.: Government Printing Office.

Le Monde (1972a) Article (January 26).

––– (1972b) Article (January 13).

––– (1971a) Article (July 6).

––– (1971b) Article (April 25).

––– (1969a) Article (November 19).

––– (1969b) Article (November 12).

––– (1969c) Article (June 13).

LE PULOCH (1964) "L'avenir des armées de terre." Revue de Défense Nationale (June): 947-960.

MARTIN, A. (1964) "L'armée de l'air dans le contexte nucléaire." Revue de Défense Nationale (October): 1499-1517.

MARTIN, L. (1969) "The great missile defense debate." Interplay (June-July).

MOUNTBATTEN (1970) Letter to The Times (February 23).

NATO Letter (1969) (September): 24-29.

NEKRASOV (1963) "Contrary to the times and to good sense." Pravda (January 19).

PIERRE, A. J. (1972) Nuclear Politics: The British Experience with an Independent Strategic Force 1939-1970. London: Oxford Univ. Press.

PLANCHAIS, J. (1965) Article in Le Monde. (January 19).

POMPIDOU, G. (1972) "Entry talks should succeed." European Community 6 (June).

––– (1971) Presidential Press Conference–Referendum on European Policy. France (March): 3.

SCHEEL, W. (1972) From a press conference. "Bonn will keine EWG soldaten." Frankfurter Rundschau (January 26).

––– (1969) Statement in the Bundestag. Bulletin (November 14).

SCHEINMAN, L. (1965) Atomic Energy Policy in France under the Fourth Republic. Princeton: Princeton Univ. Press.

SCHMIDT, H. (1962) Defense or Retaliation: A German View. New York: Praeger.

SMART, IAN (1971) Future Conditional: The Prospect for Anglo-French Nuclear Cooperation. London: International Institute for Strategic Studies.

STRAUSS, F. J. (1968) Heransfurderung und Autwort. Stuttgart: Seewala.

––– (1966) The Grand Design. Praeger.

United States Agency for International Development (1972) Gross National Product, Growth Rates and Trend. (May 10).

WILLIAMS, F. (1961) A Prime Minister Remembers. London: Heinemann.